FREE VIDEO   FREE   FREE VIDEO

Essential Test Tips Video from Trivium Test Prep

Dear Customer,

Thank you for purchasing from Trivium Test Prep! We're honored to help you prepare for your ILTS ELA exam.

To show our appreciation, we're offering a **FREE *ILTS ELA Essential Test Tips* Video by Trivium Test Prep**.* Our video includes 35 test preparation strategies that will make you successful on the ILTS ELA. All we ask is that you email us your feedback and describe your experience with our product. Amazing, awful, or just so-so: we want to hear what you have to say!

To receive your **FREE *ILTS ELA Essential Test Tips* Video**, please email us at 5star@triviumtestprep.com. Include "Free 5 Star" in the subject line and the following information in your email:

1. The title of the product you purchased.
2. Your rating from 1 – 5 (with 5 being the best).
3. Your feedback about the product, including how our materials helped you meet your goals and ways in which we can improve our products.
4. Your full name and shipping address so we can send your **FREE *ILTS ELA Essential Test Tips* Video**.

If you have any questions or concerns please feel free to contact us directly at 5star@triviumtestprep.com.

Thank you!

- Trivium Test Prep Team

*To get access to the free video please email us at 5star@triviumtestprep.com, and please follow the instructions above.

ILTS English Language Arts (207) Exam Study Guide:

2 Practice Tests and Illinois Licensure Testing System ELA Prep

3rd Edition

J.G. Cox

Copyright © 2023 by Cirrus Test Prep

ISBN-13- 9781637985892

ALL RIGHTS RESERVED. By purchase of this book, you have been licensed one copy for personal use only. No part of this work may be reproduced, redistributed, or used in any form or by any means without prior written permission of the publisher and copyright owner. Cirrus Test Prep; Trivium Test Prep; Accepted, Inc.; and Ascencia Test Prep are all imprints of Trivium Test Prep, LLC.

Pearson Education, Inc. was not involved in the creation or production of this product, is not in any way affiliated with Cirrus Test Prep, and does not sponsor or endorse this product. All test names (and their acronyms) are trademarks of their respective owners. This study guide is for general information only and does not claim endorsement by any third party.

Image(s) used under license from Shutterstock.com

About the Authors

Dr. Judith R. Coats has twenty-two years of experience teaching English in higher education and at the high school level. Specializing in grammar and writing, she has taught Advanced Grammar, Fundamentals of Composition, Composition and Research, and Research Writing. She has also taught directed study courses online including Short Story and Young Adult Literature.

Dr. Coats earned her MA in English/Writing from Northern Michigan University in 2002 and her EdD in 2012 at Regent University in Virginia. There, her research focused on the Reed and Kellogg System of sentence diagramming and implementing the system in higher education with adult learners. She has taught in Haiti and Canada and is the author of several published articles and works of fiction.

Pamela VanderVeen has thirty-one years of classroom experience in reading and high school English. She began her career as a Title I Reading teacher and went on to teach fourth grade for three years and high school English for twenty-six years. Currently, she is Coordinator of Curriculum, Instruction, and Assessment at the Forbush School in Baltimore, Maryland, where she supports teachers with curriculum materials, familiarizes teachers with the Common Core Standards, helps them implement related curricula, monitors classroom instruction, and provides progress assessments.

Ms. VanderVeen was awarded her MA in Education from the University of Delaware in 1995. She has written and published educational materials for twenty-four years, including instructional units, activities, and practice assessments. She has written ancillary materials for many texts, conducted editorial work, and correlated materials to state standards.

Table of Contents

Online Resources i
Introduction iii
1. Reading Literary Text 1
2. Reading Informational Texts 59
3. Language 83
4. Writing and Research 113
5. Speaking, Listening, and Viewing 133
6. Assessment and Instruction 151
7. Practice Test 177

Online Resources

Cirrus Test Prep includes online resources with the purchase of this study guide to help you fully prepare for your ILTS English Language Arts exam.

Practice Test
In addition to the practice test included in this book, we also offer an online exam. Since many exams today are computer based, practicing your test-taking skills on the computer is a great way to prepare.

Flash Cards
Cirrus Test Prep's flash cards allow you to review important terms easily on your computer or smartphone.

Cheat Sheets
Review the core skills you need to master the exam with easy-to-read Cheat Sheets.

From Stress to Success
Watch "From Stress to Success," a brief but insightful YouTube video that offers the tips, tricks, and secrets experts use to score higher on the exam.

Reviews
Leave a review, send us helpful feedback, or sign up for Cirrus promotions—including free books!

Access these materials at:
www.cirrustestprep.com/ilts-ela-online-resources

Introduction

Congratulations on choosing to take the Illinois Licensure Testing System: English Language Arts (207) exam! By purchasing this book, you've taken the first step toward becoming an ELA teacher.

This guide provides you with a detailed overview of the ILTS: ELA exam, so you will know exactly what to expect on test day. We'll take you through all of the concepts covered on the exam and give you the opportunity to evaluate your knowledge with practice questions. Even if it's been a while since you last took a major test, don't worry; we'll make sure you're more than ready!

What is the ILTS?

The ILTS is a testing program that assesses an examinee's knowledge and skills in accordance with professionally accepted standards of teaching. The ILTS website, www.il.nesinc.com, contains information detailing the role of the ILTS tests in determining your teaching certification application.

What's on the ILTS ELA exam?

The ILTS ELA exam is a multiple-choice test that assesses whether you possess the knowledge and skills necessary to become a secondary school ELA teacher. You will have **three hours and fifteen minutes** to answer **100 multiple-choice questions**. The approximate number of questions from each content category is shown in the table below.

What's on the ILTS ELA exam?

Subarea	Number of Scored Questions	Number of Unscored Questions	Percent of Test Score
Reading Comprehension	22	6	28%
Reading Literary and Informational Texts	18	4	22%
Writing and Research	31	8	39%
Speaking, Listening, and Viewing	9	2	11%
Total	**80**	**20**	**100%**

There is no penalty for guessing on the ELA, so be sure to eliminate answer options and respond to every question. If you still do not know the answer, guess; you may get it right!

How is the ILTS ELA exam administered?

The ILTS tests are administered at Pearson VUE testing centers across the nation. To register for the exam, go to www.il.nesinc.com. At this site, you can create an ILTS account, check testing dates, register for a test, and find instructions for registering via mail or phone. The ILTS website allows you to take a practice tutorial to acclimate yourself to the computerized format.

How is the ILTS ELA exam scored?

On the ELA, the number of correctly answered questions is used to create your scaled score, which ranges from 100 – 300. **A passing score is 240.** Score reports will be available approximately two weeks after the last day of your testing period.

About Cirrus Test Prep

Cirrus Test Prep study guides are designed by current and former educators and are tailored to meet your needs as an incoming educator. Our guides offer all of the resources necessary to help you pass teacher certification tests across the nation.

Cirrus clouds are graceful, wispy, and characterized by their high altitude. Just like cirrus clouds, Cirrus Test Prep's goal is to help educators "aim high" when it comes to obtaining their teacher certifications and entering the classroom. We're pleased you've chosen Cirrus to be a part of your professional journey!

Reading Literary Text

CONSTRUCTIVISM

In today's English classrooms, teachers are equipping students for success by devoting the bulk of their time to reading and discussing a variety of texts. This interactive approach to reading instruction (as opposed to a lecture-based approach, for example) is based on the theory of **constructivism**:

- ▶ As readers become involved with a text, they construct meaning through an active process of integrating what they are reading with their own reactions, knowledge, beliefs, and ideas.

- ▶ The constructivist perspective is linked to studies in cognition; constructivists are interested in the thinking processes readers use to comprehend and interpret text.

Many variables affect how people understand what they are reading, including prior knowledge of the subject of the text, mental schemas and assumptions, and motivation levels. For example, the extent of a reader's experience with narrative structures might determine how effectively the reader can follow the events of a new story:

- ▶ Those who are familiar with the logical structures of an argument may be better able to process the reasoning of persuasive text.

- ▶ Those who take time to understand, revisit, and reflect on the piece of writing will likely have a deeper understanding of it than a more casual reader.

> **HELPFUL HINT**
>
> **Schemas** are cognitive connections that are molded in an individual's mind over time and shape a person's worldview. Knowledge is stored as a complex web of schemas; learning occurs when new information links to existing schematic networks.

Constructivism also places emphasis on how the social and cultural backgrounds of readers influence how they understand and experience a text. For example, when reading the introduction to Alice Walker's short story "Everyday Use," White, middle class students who have grown up in the urban areas of northern states may struggle to relate to a mom who wears overalls and kills hogs. Generally, students who have experiences that mirror the details of the text to some degree are better able to make meaningful personal connections with it.

IMPORTANT WORKS

"Everyday Use"
Author: Alice Walker
Publication Date: 1973
Summary: In this short story, Mama considers the past, including a fire that burned her daughter Maggie. She awaits the arrival of her other daughter, Dee, who has had a different life from her mother and sister after being sent away to school. Dee arrives with Hakim-a-barber, her boyfriend, and explains that she does not want to be called Dee anymore, saying that her oppressors gave her that name; she now goes by Wangero. Her mother explains that she was named after her grandmother and many others before her but agrees to call her Wangero. The family begins to eat, but Hakim-a-barber, a Muslim, cannot eat the collard greens and pork. After asking for some kitchen objects used to make butter, Dee finds two quilts made by her grandmother, aunts, and mother in Mama's trunk; she asks if she can have them. Mama says that they have already been promised to Maggie, but Dee advocates for the quilts, noting that she doesn't think Maggie—who is not as learned and worldly as she is—will know how to care for them. Though Maggie offers to give the quilts to her sister, Mama refuses. Dee suggests that her mother does not understand her heritage and that she and Maggie should make something better out of their lives. She drives off with her boyfriend, and Maggie and Mama stay in the yard enjoying the evening.
Themes, Motifs, and Symbols: family history and connectedness; heritage, race, and identity; education as a divisive force

Constructivists also emphasize that most learning and understanding occur in a social context. In other words, readers are better able to construct interpretations of and find meaning in a text when they have opportunities to engage in dialogue about it with others.

For example, in an English classroom, a teacher might initiate a discussion with an open-ended, text-based question:

- ▶ Student A may answer with an assertion and simple explanation.
- ▶ Student B might disagree and explain her reasoning.
- ▶ Student A can then respond by elaborating on his original idea.

Other students listening to this collision of thought can begin to examine the merits of each position and perhaps, after a prompt from the teacher, return to the text to look for evidence to contribute to the discussion. Students might even revise their original interpretations when they are confronted by the ideas of others.

During such open discussions, students not only deepen their understandings of the text but also practice critical thinking and effective ways of communicating ideas.

The main implication of constructivist theory for reading instruction is that teachers should design lessons that require students to both respond to and interact with text as they read as well as interact with each other through authentic discussion and debate. Activities that provide opportunities for students to process, share, and examine their thoughts about texts are essential.

> **HELPFUL HINT**
>
> **Transactional reading**, or **transactional reader-response theory**, was first developed by Louise Rosenblatt. This theory states that text on a page is nothing until it becomes a performance of meaning in the reader's mind. An individual's interpretation of a text gives it meaning.

PRACTICE QUESTION

1) Which of the following is NOT a way that class discussions support the constructivist theory of reading instruction?

    A. They offer students a chance to hear the ideas of their fellow students and increase their knowledge of diverse viewpoints.

    B. They provide students practice with social interaction by forcing them to listen to others and respect alternative opinions.

    C. They challenge students to use concrete evidence, which enhances their knowledge and memory of the text.

    D. They give students the opportunity to express their interpretations, consider any alternative viewpoints, and examine their ideas in terms of the evidence that is mentioned.

LITERARY TRADITIONS

Not all texts can be classified as literature. In vague terms, creative writers write to entertain; however, the goal of authors, poets, and playwrights is rarely that simple.

Literary texts, especially when written well, have the capacity to create an experience for the reader by using language to reflect universal aspects of life or human nature. The power of language—in the form of literature—to elicit interpretive responses in readers has given rise to the field of **literary criticism**, the formal study, analysis, and evaluation of literary texts.

The field of literary criticism continually shapes English literature courses. A critical approach to literature—which takes into account historical, philosophical, cultural, and social traditions—lends itself easily to valuable interdisciplinary instruction.

Effective teachers set a clear purpose, some guiding questions, and a logical structure for their course; they also select texts purposefully, taking into account each text's origin, relevance, and canonicity.

American Literature

> **HELPFUL HINT**
>
> In literature, a **canon** is a group of works that are considered to be culturally, artistically, or historically significant. *Canonicity*, therefore, refers to whether the work is considered important enough to be a part of the broad literature canon.

American literature includes works from the early colonial period through the present and is generally divided into five categories. The periods themselves, the specific range of years, and the authors associated with them continue to be debated among scholars, which is why some of them overlap. Many scholars consider the Civil War to be a turning point in American literature and a stand-alone era of literature; as such this has been added as a sixth literary period to this list.

Various subperiods exist loosely within these periods, each with its own characteristics:

The Colonial and Early National period (seventeenth century – ca. 1830)

- The Revolutionary period (ca. 1765 – ca.1790)

The Romantic period (ca. 1830 – ca. 1870)

- Transcendentalism (late 1820s – early 1850s)

Civil War period (ca. 1855 – ca. 1870)

Realism (ca. 1870 – ca. 1910)

- Naturalism (late nineteenth century; ca. 1880 – ca. 1915)
- Regionalism (late nineteenth and early twentieth centuries; ca. 1865 – ca. 1920)

The Modernist period (ca. 1910 – ca. 1945)

- Harlem Renaissance (ca. 1918 – ca. 1937)
- The Lost Generation (ca. 1920 – ca. 1950)

The Contemporary period (ca. 1945 – present)

The Colonial and Early National Period (Seventeenth Century – ca. 1830)

Texts from this period represent the earliest American literature and center on exploration and life in the New World. Writings from this time often focus on the future, especially in the lead-up to the American Revolution and after the US declared its independence in 1776. **The Revolutionary period** (ca. 1765 – ca. 1790), which is characterized by politically motivated writings, is included in this literary time frame. Writing styles from this period tend to be practical and straightforward.

Table 1.1. Important Writers of the Colonial and Early National Period and Its Subperiod

Colonial and Early National Period
seventeenth century – ca. 1830

Author	Title
William Bradford	*Of Plymouth Plantation*
Anne Bradstreet	*The Tenth Muse Lately Sprung Up in America*, various poetry
Jonathan Edwards	"Sinners in the Hands of an Angry God"
Olaudah Equiano	*The Interesting Narrative of the Life of Olaudah Equiano*

The Revolutionary Period
ca. 1765 – ca.1790

Author	Title(s)
Benjamin Franklin	*Poor Richard's Almanack*
Thomas Jefferson	*Notes on the State of Virginia*, various letters
James Madison	the "Federalist Papers" (with Alexander Hamilton and John Jay), most of the US Constitution
Thomas Paine	*Common Sense* and various essays

The Romantic Period (ca. 1830 – ca. 1870)

Writing from this period emphasizes individuals rather than groups and emotional experience rather than reason; value is placed on nature. Texts concerning both enslaved and free African Americans increased in the years up to, during, and following the Civil War. The Romantic period also includes **Transcendentalism** (late 1820s – early 1850s), which describes

> **DID YOU KNOW?**
>
> The sermon "Sinners in the Hands of an Angry God" (Jonathan Edwards) is considered to be the catalyst for the First Great Awakening.

a subperiod of literature based on the philosophy that all of creation is part of a unified whole. Transcendentalist writings value self-reliance and are marked by a belief in the inherent goodness of both people and the natural world around them.

Table 1.2. Important Writers of the Romantic Period and Its Subperiod

The Romantic Period
ca. 1830 – ca. 1870

Author	Title(s)
James Fenimore Cooper	*The Last of the Mohicans*
Washington Irving	"The Devil and Tom Walker"
Edgar Allan Poe	"The Raven," "The Tell-Tale Heart," other various short stories and poetry
Sojourner Truth	"Ain't I a Woman"

Transcendentalism
late 1820s – early 1850s

Author	Title(s)
Ralph Waldo Emerson	*Self-Reliance* and *The American Scholar*
Henry David Thoreau	*Walden* and *Civil Disobedience*
Walt Whitman	"Song of Myself," "Oh Captain! My Captain!"

CIVIL WAR PERIOD (CA. 1855 – CA. 1870)

Works from this time are considered by many scholars to be a turning point in American literature. Ideals expressed during the Romantic period were tested, and a new generation of writers emerged. Writings from this time are often narrative and include diaries and political speeches.

Table 1.3. Important Writers of the Civil War Period (ca. 1855 – ca. 1870)

Author	Title(s)
Mary Chesnut	*Diary of Mary Chesnut (A Diary from Dixie)*
Frederick Douglass	*My Bondage and My Freedom*
Abraham Lincoln	"The Gettysburg Address"

REALISM (CA. 1870 – CA. 1910)

Inspired by the immense toll of the country's recent Civil War, authors during this period aimed to portray American life as it truly was. **Naturalism** (late nineteenth century) was considered an especially intense form of realism that supported ideas of determinism, scientific objectivism, and detachment. Regionalist authors are yet another subperiod. Also known as "local color," **Regionalism** (late nineteenth – early twentieth centuries) is characterized by a heavy focus on a region (dialect, history, customs, and so forth). Increasing societal changes as a result of the Civil War and continued westward expansion helped fuel the regionalist style of writing.

> **DID YOU KNOW?**
>
> Sojourner Truth delivered her speech "Ain't I a Woman" at the 1851 Women's Rights Convention in Akron, Ohio. It remains among the most notable women's rights and abolitionist speeches in US history.

Table 1.4. Important Writers of the Realism Period and Its Subperiods

The Realism Period
ca. 1870 – ca. 1910

Author	Title(s)
William Dean Howells	writer and editor of the *Atlantic Monthly*
Mark Twain	*The Adventures of Huckleberry Finn,* various essays

Naturalism
late nineteenth century

Author	Title(s)
Kate Chopin	*The Awakening*
Jack London	*The Call of the Wild*
John Steinbeck	*The Grapes of Wrath*

Regionalism
late nineteenth century

Author	Title(s)
Willa Cather	*My Antonia*
William Faulkner	*Absalom! Absalom!*

THE MODERNIST PERIOD (CA. 1910 – CA. 1945)

The progress made possible by advancements in science and technology collided with the suffering brought about by World War I and the Great Depression, ushering in the **Modernist period** of literature. This set the stage for the modernist movement, defined as a radical break from the past. Characteristics of writings from this period include disillusionment and a sense of loss that range from destructive impulses to hope that change is imminent.

The **Harlem Renaissance (ca. 1918 – ca. 1937)**, considered the most influential movement in African American literary history, is one subperiod of this time.

Writings are characterized by relationships to civil rights and reform organizations with a goal of shifting how Black culture was represented. It includes literary as well as musical, theatrical, and visual arts.

The Lost Generation (ca. 1920 – ca. 1950) describes a generation of authors who largely came of age in the years leading up to and including World War I and the early 1920s. Characteristics of this subperiod include disillusionment, uncertainty about the future, and loss of identity.

Table 1.5. Important Writers of the Modernist Period and Its Subperiods

The Modernist Period
ca. 1910 – ca. 1945

Author	Title(s)
E.E. Cummings	*The Enormous Room,* various poetry
Robert Frost	*A Boy's Will, North of Boston*
Sinclair Lewis	*Babbitt, Main Street*
Margaret Mitchell	*Gone with the Wind*
Flannery O'Connor	*Wise Blood,* various short stories
Katherine Porter	*Ship of Fools,* various short stories
Ezra Pound	*Ripostes, Hugh Selwyn Mauberley*
Eudora Welty	*The Optimist's Daughter*
Edith Wharton	*The Age of Innocence*
Tennessee Williams	*A Streetcar Named Desire, The Glass Menagerie,* other plays

The Harlem Renaissance
ca. 1918 – ca. 1937

Author	Title(s)
Countee Cullen	"Yet Do I Marvel," various poems
Langston Hughes	"Mother to Son," various poems
Zora Neale Hurston	*Their Eyes Were Watching God*

The Lost Generation
ca. 1920 – ca. 1950

Author	Title(s)
T.S. Eliot	"The Love Song of J. Alfred Prufrock," other poetry and plays
F. Scott Fitzgerald	*The Great Gatsby, Tender Is the Night,* other works
Ernest Hemingway	*The Old Man and the Sea, A Farewell to Arms, For Whom the Bell Tolls,* other works
Gertrude Stein	*The Autobiography of Alice B. Toklas, Tender Buttons,* other works

The Contemporary Period (1945 – present)

Writing during the **Contemporary period** often reflects the political and cultural shifts of the times. The prospect of nuclear war, the Civil Rights Movement, women's rights, and a growing focus on equality shape this period of American literature.

Table 1.6. Important Writers of the Contemporary Period (1945 – present)

Author	Title(s)
Sandra Cisneros	*The House on Mango Street*
Don DiLillo	*White Noise*
Nikki Giovanni	*Black Feeling, Black Talk, Black Judgement,* other works
Joseph Heller	*Catch-22*
Ursula K. Le Guin	*The Left Hand of Darkness*
Martin Luther King	*"I Have A Dream,"* various speeches and letters
Cormac McCarthy	*The Road, No Country for Old Men*
J.D. Salinger	*The Catcher in the Rye*
Amy Tan	*The Joy Luck Club*
John Updike	*Rabbit, Run*
Kurt Vonnegut	*Slaughterhouse-Five, Cat's Cradle*
Alice Walker	*The Color Purple*
August Wilson	*The Pittsburgh Cycle*
Richard Wright	*Black Boy*

PRACTICE QUESTION

2) This text provides a factually accurate account of the Civil War; in writing it, the author observed and recorded descriptions of and reactions to events of the war. The text is subjective, told from the first person point of view, and filled with the details that impressed the writer. As it reveals the personal responses of a person in the midst of turmoil, it offers insights into the occurrences and effects of the Civil War.

   What text does the passage describe?

   A. *"Oh Captain! My Captain!"* (Walt Whitman)
   B. *The Diary of Mary Chesnut* (Mary Chesnut)
   C. *The Gettysburg Address* (Abraham Lincoln)
   D. *My Bondage and My Freedom* (Frederick Douglass)

DID YOU KNOW?

Across the centuries, the prevailing themes of American literature include individualism, the American dream/reality, cultural diversity, tolerance, and the search for identity.

British Literature

British literature comprises the literary texts of the British Isles. The literature of Great Britain tends to reflect changes in culture and thinking over time and is therefore usually studied chronologically by period. Like American literature, subperiods with their own unique characteristics exist within these larger literary periods. The specific breakdown of these periods and the years associated with them continue to be debated among scholars.

1. The Anglo-Saxon (Old English) period (ca. 450 – ca. 1066)
2. The Middle English (Medieval) period (ca. 1066 – ca. 1500)
3. The Renaissance (ca. 1500 – ca. 1660)
   - The Elizabethan Age (ca. 1558 – ca. 1603)
   - The Jacobean Age (ca. 1603 – ca. 1625)
   - The Caroline Age (ca. 1625 – ca. 1649); includes the Metaphysical poets (ca. 1600 – ca. 1690), who especially flourished during this time
   - The Commonwealth period (ca. 1649 – ca. 1660)
4. The Neoclassical Period (ca. 1600 – ca. 1785)
   - The Restoration (ca. 1660 – ca. 1700)
   - The Augustan Age (ca. 1700 – ca. 1745)
   - The Age of Sensibility (ca. 1745 – ca. 1785)
   - The Enlightenment (ca. 1600 – ca. 1800)
5. The Romantic period (ca. 1785 – ca. 1832)
6. The Victorian period (ca. 1832 – ca. 1901)
7. The Modern period (ca. 1901 – ca. 1945)
   - The Edwardian (ca. 1901 – ca. 1914) and Georgian (ca. 1910 – ca. 1936) periods overlap with the Modern period.
8. The Postmodern period (ca. 1945 onward)

The Anglo-Saxon (Old English) Period (ca. 450 – ca. 1066)

The first period of recorded texts is the **Anglo-Saxon**, or **Old English**, period. Oral literature dominated the first half of this literary period until roughly the seventh century. Literature from this time is marked by epic poems about courageous heroes; their concern was morality and goodness. Other works were often translations of legal, medical, or religious prose.

Table 1.7. Important Writers of the Anglo-Saxon (Old English) Period (ca. 450 – ca. 1066)

Author	Title(s)
Cædmon	"Cædmon's Hymn"
Cynewulf	"The Fates of the Apostles"
unknown/anonymous	"Beowulf"
unknown/anonymous	"The Wife's Lament"
unknown/anonymous	"The Seafarer"

THE MIDDLE ENGLISH PERIOD (CA. 1066 – CA. 1500)

The **Middle English**, or **Medieval**, period witnessed a major language, lifestyle, and culture shift that formed the foundation of the English language that is recognized today. Works from this period focus on religion, romance, diversity, and chivalry. Morality plays and folk ballads were also popular during this time.

> **DID YOU KNOW?**
>
> Many scholars consider *The Book of Margery Kempe* to be the first autobiography written in the English language.

Table 1.8. Important Writers of the Middle English (Medieval) Period (ca. 1066 – ca. 1500)

Author	Title(s)
Chaucer	*The Canterbury Tales*
Margery Kempe	*The Book of Margery Kempe*
Sir Thomas Malory	*Le Morte d'Arthur*

THE RENAISSANCE (CA. 1500 – CA. 1660)

The **Renaissance** is marked by a *rebirth* (taken from the French translation for *renaissance*) of Classical values and learning. It is divided into four subperiods, with authors and their works often overlapping.

The **Elizabethan Age** (ca. 1558 – ca. 1603) is known as the golden age English drama and public theatres. **The Jacobean Age** (ca. 1603 – ca. 1625) describes literary and other arts under the reign of James VI of Scotland. **Metaphysical poets** (ca. 1600 – ca. 1690), whose works often focus on philosophical exploration, flourished during the **Caroline Age** (ca. 1625 – ca. 1649), which is often referred to as the "age of poetry." Finally, the **Commonwealth period** (ca. 1649 – ca. 1660) marked the end of the English Civil War and the start of a Puritan-led Parliament during which public theaters closed in response to perceived transgressions—moral and otherwise. Political writings also began to appear during this period.

Table 1.9. Important Writers of the Renaissance

The Elizabethan Age
ca. 1558 – ca. 1603

Author	Title(s)
Ben Jonson	*Every Man in His Humour*
Christopher Marlowe	*Dido, Queen of Carthage*
William Shakespeare	*Romeo and Juliet, Hamlet, Macbeth*
Edmund Spenser	*The Faerie Queene*

The Jacobean Age
ca. 1603 – ca. 1625

Author	Title(s)
Francis Bacon	*Advancement of Learning*
Robert Burton	*The Anatomy of Melancholy*

Metaphysical Poets of the Caroline Age
ca. 1625 – ca. 1649

Author	Title(s)
John Donne	"The Flea," various poems
George Herbert	"Easter Wings"
Andrew Marvell	"To His Coy Mistress," various poems

The Commonwealth Period
ca. 1649 – ca. 1660

Author	Title(s)
Thomas Hobbes	*Leviathan*
John Milton	*Paradise Lost*

The Neoclassical Period (ca. 1600 – ca. 1785)

The **Neoclassical** period is comprised of **The Restoration** (ca. 1660 – ca. 1700), the works of which gave birth to satire and "comedies of manner" and offered a response to the return of puritanism seen during the Commonwealth period.

The **Augustan Age** (ca. 1700 – ca. 1745) sees female writers challenge gender stereotypes, especially concerning female roles. The **Age of Sensibility** (ca. 1745 – ca. 1785), also known as the "Age of Johnson," embraces ideas of neoclassicism (art inspired by classic antiquity) and the **Enlightenment** (ca. 1600 – ca. 1800) an outlook on the world shared by many intellectuals of the time that emphasizes logic, reason, and rules.

Table 1.10. Important Writers of the Neoclassical Period

The Restoration
ca. 1660 – ca. 1700

Author	Title(s)
John Bunyan	*The Pilgrim's Progress*
Samuel Butler	*Hudibras*
William Congreve	*The Old Bachelor, The Way of the World*
John Dryden	*Absalom and Achitophel*

The Augustan Age
ca. 1700 – ca. 1745

Author	Title(s)
Alexander Pope	*The Dunciad*
Jonathan Swift	*Gulliver's Travels*

The Age of Sensibility
ca. 1745 – ca. 1785

Author	Title(s)
James Boswell	*Life of Johnson* also known as *Life of Samuel Johnson*
Edmund Burke	*A Vindication of Natural Society*
Samuel Johnson	*The Dictionary of the English Language*

The Enlightenment
ca. 1600 – ca. 1800

Author	Title(s)
John Locke	*A Letter Concerning Toleration, An Essay Concerning Human Understanding*
Montesquieu	*The Persian Letters,* various memoirs and discourses at the Academy of Bordeaux
Jean Jacques Rosseau	*The Social Contract, Discourse on the Arts and Sciences*

THE ROMANTIC PERIOD (CA. 1785 – CA. 1832)

Works from the **Romantic** period are diverse, arguably the most well-known, and characterized by a focus on feelings and the imagination. The French Revolution and the Industrial Revolution influenced many of the writers of this time, who believed truth was found in nature and unrestrained imaginative experience. Many poems and lyrical ballads were written, as well as gothic horror novels.

Table 1.11 Important Writers of the Romantic Period (ca. 1785 – ca. 1832)

Author	Title(s)
Lord Byron	"Don Juan"
John Keats	"Hyperion," "Isabella"
Percy Bysshe Shelley	"Ode to the West Wind," "The Masque of Anarchy"
Mary Shelley	*Frankenstein*
William Wordsworth	"Tintern Abbey," "To the Cuckoo"

THE VICTORIAN PERIOD (CA. 1832 – CA. 1901)

The **Victorian** period was marked by social, religious, and economic turmoil; literature from this time often portrays idealized versions of life's struggles. Many scholars consider this period in writing as a bridge between the Romantic and Modern periods. A growing middle class during this time benefitted from the mass printing of novels and magazines; elegies were also popular. The Victorian, Edwardian (ca. 1901 – ca. 1914), and Georgian (ca. 1910 – ca. 1936) periods (the latter two of which overlap with the Modern period), are all named for the reigning monarchs of the time; writings often center around cultural issues specific to each of these periods.

> **DID YOU KNOW?**
>
> Percy Bysshe Shelley's "The Masque of Anarchy" is a political poem written after the Peterloo Massacre in England. It is considered one of the first statements on the idea of nonviolent resistance.

Table 1.12. Important Writers of the Victorian Period (ca. 1832 – ca. 1901)

Author	Title(s)
Elizabeth Barrett Browning	"How Do I Love Thee?" (Sonnet 43 from *Sonnets from the Portuguese*)
Robert Browning	"The Pied Piper of Hamelin," *Men and Women*
Charles Dickens	*A Tale of Two Cities, Oliver Twist*
Thomas Hardy	*The Return of the Native, Tess of d'Urbervilles*
Rudyard Kipling	*The Jungle Book*
Alfred Tennyson	"Ulysses"

THE MODERN PERIOD (CA. 1901 – CA. 1945)

Writers of the **Modern** period often focus on social issues in which characters experience epiphanies. Novelists were known to play with style during this time by writing in a stream of consciousness. As noted earlier, works from the Edwardian and Georgian periods often overlap with the Modern period.

Table 1.13. Important Writers of the Modern Period (ca. 1901 – ca. 1945)

Author	Title(s)
Joseph Conrad	*Heart of Darkness*
T. S. Eliot	*The Waste Land,* various poems
D. H. Lawrence	*Women in Love*
Katherine Mansfield	"The Garden Party," various short stories
George Orwell	*Animal Farm*
Bernard Shaw	*Pygmalion*
Dylan Thomas	"Do Not Go Gentle Into That Good Night," various poems
Virginia Woolf	*Mrs. Dalloway,* various stories
William Yeats	"When You Are Old," various poems

THE POSTMODERN PERIOD (CA. 1945 ONWARD)

Some scholars note the emergence of the Postmodern period after World War II; it is often understood to be a response to modernism. By the late twentieth century, writers had become interested in psychology, criticism, and the close observation of human behaviors and relationships.

DID YOU KNOW?

Elizabeth Barrett Browning's famous "How Do I Love Thee?" poem is actually one of several untitled poems from her larger work *Sonnets from the Portuguese*, the title of which served as a code to her husband, Robert Browning, for whom these love sonnets were written.

Table 1.14. Important Writers of the Postmodern Period (ca. 1945 onward)

Author	Title(s)
Doris Lessing	*The Golden Notebook*
Penelope Lively	*The Road to Lichfield, A Stitch in Time*

PRACTICE QUESTION

3) Which of the following authors wrote during the Victorian Period? Select all that apply

    A. Charles Dickens

    B. Virginia Woolf

    C. Robert Browning

    D. John Donne

    E. William Wordsworth

WORLD LITERATURE

World literature can refer to all national literatures, but the term usually refers to a group of important representative literary works that are circulated and studied around the globe. These works come from a variety of areas including France, Africa, India, China, Japan, ancient Greece and Rome, and the ancient Middle East. The emphasis of study in a world literature course or unit is usually the cultural, philosophical, and historical context of the literary works. Sometimes, the works are grouped by commonalities, as in the study of lyrical poetry, creation myths, or hero tales; other times, selections are chosen to highlight how certain literary ideas have moved across cultures.

HELPFUL HINT

Samuel Beckett *(Waiting for Godot, Endgame)* was an Irish writer whose work straddles the Modernist and Postmodernist periods. In his early years, he worked closely with the Modernist Irish writer James Joyce *(Portrait of the Artist as a Young Man, Ulysses)*. Beckett's later works incorporated more Postmodern elements, such as fragmented narration and playful humor.

Non-Western literature is from any country other than the United States, those found in Western Europe, or ancient Greece and Rome. Some examples of authors from non-Western countries are Isabel Allende and Gabriel García Márquez from Latin America, Bessie Head and Ngũgĩ wa Thiong'o from Africa, and Rumi of Persia. Usually studies of non-Western literature focus on the contrasts between Western and non-Western perspectives with the goal of achieving familiarity with the rich histories, intellectual traditions, and cultural beliefs represented in the works. Often, studies emphasize both the interconnectedness and the diversity of cultures.

Table 1.15. Important Works in World and Non-Western Literature

Title (Author)	Country of Origin	Description
Things Fall Apart Chinua Achebe	Nigeria	depicts precolonial Nigeria and the impacts of European colonialism in the 19th century
Agamemnon Aeschylus	ancient Greece	one of three major Greek tragedies—a popular form of theatre; describes how a family is punished by the gods for a series of murders; complex religious issues often addressed by the author
House of Spirits Isabel Allende	Chile	a family saga that follows four generations and is set against the backdrop of postcolonial Chile; uses magical realism to discuss the connections between politics, memory, and Chilean culture

Title (Author)	Country of Origin	Description
The Epic of Gilgamesh Anonymous	ancient Mesopotamia	a story written as a poem on twelve clay tablets (standard Babylonian version) about a wild man created by the gods to prevent Gilgamesh from oppressing his people; Gilgamesh and his search for eternal life; considered as the foundation of heroic saga literature
The Blind Assassin *The Handmaid's Tale* Margaret Atwood	Canada	written with elements of science fiction, romance, and gothic suspense; a multilayered story concerning death and a family's history *(The Blind Assasin)*; a dystopian novel that imagines a theocratic and totalitarian state in which handmaids are forced to bear children due to low reproduction rates *(The Handmaid's Tale)*
Labyrinths Jorge Luis Borges	Argentina	a collection of short stories and essays that feature magical realism and the use of symbolism and metaphors; many recurring themes, especially concerning the concept of time
The Good Earth Pearl S. Buck	United States (written in China by an American author; modeled after Chinese novels)	the story of a farmer and his family's life in 1920s China and the political and social upheavals of that time; winner of the Pulitzer Prize
Don Quixote Miguel Cervantes	Habsburg Spain	considered a prototype for the modern novel; revolves around the adventures of a young man who hopes to become a knight, serve his country, and usher in a return to chivalry
Three Sisters *The Seagull* Anton Chekov	Russia	a play concerning three sisters who must grapple with suffering and change in their own lives against the backdrop of real-world issues taking place around them *(Three Sisters)*; a play in which the characters use subtext in dialogue; themes include unrequited love, artistic endeavors and the pursuit of fame, and ego versus self *(The Seagull)*

continued on next page

Table 1.15. Important Works in World and Non–Western Literature (cont.)

Title (Author)	Country of Origin	Description
The Alchemist Paulo Coelho	Brazil	a novel about self-discovery and individuality; known for its use of allegory
The Divine Comedy *Inferno* Dante	Italy	a narrative poem that depicts Dante's travels in the afterlife and represents a soul's journey to God (*The Divine Comedy*) discusses the author's journey through Hell; the first part of *The Divine Comedy* (*Inferno*)
The Brothers Karamazov *Crime and Punishment* Fyodor Dostoyevsky	Russia	a philosophical novel revolving around patricide set against the backdrop of a modernizing Russia with themes of morality, faith, and doubt (*The Brothers Karamazov*) written after the author's exile in Siberia; depicts the moral dilemmas and mental anguish stemming from a murder (*Crime and Punishment*)
The Count of Monte Cristo Alexandre Dumas	France	an adventure novel that takes place during the Bourbon Restoration in France and tells the story of a man who escapes an unjust incarceration to seek revenge
Like Water for Chocolate Laura Esquivel	Mexico	a story of self-growth love, tradition, rebellion, and family; employs the use of magical realism
"Medea" Euripides	ancient Greece	the second of the three major Greek tragedies; based on the myth of Medea and Jason, who leaves Medea for another woman; noted for its simplicity; examines themes of love, passion, and vengeance
The Tin Drum Gunter Grass	West Germany	the first book of Grass's *Danzig Trilogy*; narrated by a main character who lived through Nazi occupation; offers perspective on German history and the human condition
Siddhartha: An Indian Poem Herman Hesse	Germany	a novel (not an actual poem) inspired by Hesse's visit to India; describes a young Brahman's search for self-realization
The Odyssey Homer	ancient Greece	epic poem divided into twenty-four books that explores themes of wandering, returning, "guest-friendship," omens, and being tested; tells the story of Odysseus, King of Ithaca, who tries to return home after the end of the Trojan War

Title (Author)	Country of Origin	Description
The Kite Runner Khaled Hosseini	United States	takes place in Afghanistan (author's birthplace) in the midst of its turbulent history, including Soviet occupation and the rise of the Taliban; tells the story of friendship between a wealthy Afghan boy and a servant's son; themes of guilt, family, and redemption
The Hunchback of Notre Dame Victor Hugo	France	written to save Notre Dame cathedral and preserve French culture during an era of immense change; themes of determinism and architecture; original title: *Notre-Dame de Paris*
Peer Gynt Henrik Ibsen	Norway	a five-act play in verse; inspired by a fairy tale the author believed to be true; a story of youth, adventure, missteps, and eventual redemption
The Trial Franz Kafka	Germany	themes that examine the idea of justice versus law, the absence of unequivocal truth, alienation, sexuality; considered to be a criticism of totalitarian authority
One Hundred Years of Solitude *Love in the Time of Cholera* Gabriel García Márquez	Colombia	an epic family saga spanning several generations and a century's worth of Latin American history (*One Hundred Years of Solitude*) a story of two lovers reuniting; woven with themes of aging, death, and love; set in a South American community affected by war and cholera outbreaks (*Love in the Time of Cholera*)
The Wind-Up Bird Chronicle Haruki Murakami	Japan	a story about a man who looks for his wife's missing cat and discovers a netherworld beneath Tokyo; examines themes of power, desire, and alienation
Cry, the Beloved Country Alan Paton	South Africa	takes place in the lead-up to Apartheid in South Africa; employs Biblical references; considered a social protest in response to a society that would eventually usher in Apartheid; showcases the consequences of fear
All Quiet of the Western Front Erich Remarque	Germany	written by a World War I veteran; describes the extraordinary mental and physical stress endured by German soldiers during the war and the subsequent detachment they felt from civilian life; themes of blind nationalism and lost youth

continued on next page

Table 1.15. Important Works in World and Non-Western Literature (cont.)

Title (Author)	Country of Origin	Description
Midnight's Children Salman Rushdie	United Kingdom	depicts the transition of India from colonial rule to independence and the country's eventual partition; employs a self-reflexive style that weaves history with fiction
The Tale of Genji Murasaki Shikibu	Japan	early 11th century work written by a noblewoman and lady-in-waiting at the peak of the Fujiwara clan's power; considered by some to be the world's first novel; depicts aristocratic lifestyles during the Heian period through the lens of Hikaru Genji, the son of an emperor who is demoted to a commoner; themes include love, lust, and family loyalty
"Antigone" Sophocles	ancient Greece	the third of the three major Greek tragedies; describes the tale of a woman who buries her brother in defiance of an order from the king; examines themes of family loyalty, blindness versus sight, fate, free will, mortality, and civil disobedience
Anna Karenina *War and Peace* Leo Tolstoy	Russia	takes place during an age of liberal reform brought about by Emperor Alexander II of Russia; examines Imperial Russian society and themes of faith, betrayal, desire, and family *(Anna Karenina)* weaves history with philosophy; discusses the French invasion of Russia and the effects of the Napoleonic era on Tsarist society; includes themes of religion, patriotism, forgiveness, and pacifism *(War and Peace)*
Night *Dawn* Elie Wiesel	Buenos Aires, Argentina: Central Union of Polish Jews in Argentina *(Night)* France, US, UK *(Dawn)*	a memoir based on the author's experiences with his father in a Nazi German concentration camp; includes themes of lost faith, guilt, inhumanity, and the relationship between fathers and sons *(Night)* a novel about a Holocaust survivor who relocates to the British Mandate of Palestine, joins a paramilitary group, and is tasked with executing a British author; explores themes of past versus present and the internal struggle of becoming someone you despise *(Dawn)*

PRACTICE QUESTION

4) Which of the following texts could be included in a unit that explores the effects of colonialism from an Indigenous peoples' perspective? Select all that apply.

   A. Gunter Grass's *The Tin Drum*
   B. Chinua Achebe's *Things Fall Apart*
   C. Haruki Murakami's *The Wind-Up Bird Chronicle*
   D. Isabel Allende's *House of Spirits*
   E. Khaled Hosseini's *The Kite Runner*

> **DID YOU KNOW?**
>
> Elie Wiesel's *The Night Trilogy* consists of three books: *Night, Dawn,* and *Day.*

YOUNG ADULT LITERATURE

Young adult literature includes texts written for adolescent readers, youth up to age twenty-five. Usually, the texts are fictional, problem novels, and romances; however nonfiction, poetry, graphic novels, and comics are popular as well. Young adult literature aims to be relevant to young people, to address their needs and interests, and to allow them to see themselves in the stories. Typical themes involve dealing with social issues, answering moral and ethical questions, relating to others, finding acceptance while maintaining uniqueness, and discovering one's individual identity.

Table 1.16. Important Young Adult Works

Title (Author)	Country of Origin	Description
Tuck Everlasting Natalie Babbitt	United States	a story about immortality; a young girl discovers a family who drank from a spring that granted them eternal youth prompting another character to attempt to exploit this knowledge; uses symbolism
Are You There, God? It's Me, Margaret Judy Blume	United States	the story of a sixth-grade girl who is seeking a single religion while dealing with the everyday experiences of being an adolescent girl
The Hunger Games (series) Suzanne Collins	United States	dystopian works that take place in a post-apocalyptic nation; themes include the origins and effects of war, distrust of authority, and class discrimination; told through the eyes of a teen protagonist

Table 1.16. Important Young Adult Works (continued)

Title (Author)	Country of Origin	Description
Lord of the Flies William Golding	United Kingdom	the tale of a group of British boys who are stranded on an island and their attempts to govern themselves; examines themes of individuality groupthink, rational versus emotional, and morality versus immorality
The Outsiders S.E. Hinton	United States	written when the author was a teen; a story about rival gangs from different socioeconomic classes; explores themes of family dysfunction, identity, self-sacrifice, honor, and empathy
Flowers for Algernon Daniel Keyes	United States	a short story turned novel about a lab mouse who has surgery to boost his intelligence; narrated as progress reports by the first human to undergo the same surgery; includes themes of the treatment of the mentally disabled, intellect versus emotion, and how the past affects the present; uses the science fiction theme of "uplift"
The Giver Lois Lowry	United States	a dystopian novel about a society that eradicates emotion and contention and the boy who is selected to store all of society's past memories; explores themes of individuality, memory, rules, control, freedom, and choice
Anne of Green Gables L.M. Montgomery	United States (published) Canada (written)	set on Prince Edward Island, Canada; the story of an orphaned girl mistakenly sent to live with her older siblings and the trials and tribulations she experiences as she grows up in her new town; examines themes of
Hatchet Gary Paulsen	United States	a wilderness survival novel; the first in a series; the story of a young teen who crash lands in the wilderness of Canada and his fight to survive; explores themes of man and nature, wisdom versus knowledge, transformation, family, and perseverance

Title (Author)	Country of Origin	Description
Harry Potter (series) J.K. Rowling	United Kingdom	a fantasy series; the life and times of a young wizard and his friends who study at a school for witchcraft and wizardry and their struggle against a dark wizard; themes include death, loss, love, corruption, and prejudice
The Catcher in the Rye J.D. Salinger	United States	a coming-of-age novel about a teen who has been expelled from his prep school; takes place over the course of about three days; themes include identity, alienation, sex, and the author's perception of phoniness in the world around him

PRACTICE QUESTION

The book introduces a world without color, joy, or fear, in which a single person holds the memories of the community's history. When a young boy is selected to become the new Receiver of Memory, he must decide if he wants his community to know the truth.

5) The passage above discusses

    A. Lois Lowry's *The Giver*

    B. Gary Paulsen's *Hatchet*

    C. William Golding's *Lord of the Flies*

    D. Suzanne Collins's *The Hunger Games*

IMPORTANT WORKS

Civil Disobedience

Author: Henry David Thoreau

Publication Date: 1849

Summary: The work is a critique of the American government's response to slavery and the Mexican War. Thoreau explains that government itself is not necessarily a good thing, and the majority, who rules any government, may be wrong. He notes that people are not required to obey unjust laws and must follow their own sense of morality. He calls on people to refuse to participate in the unjust US government lest they further perpetuate its evils. He argues that attempting to enact change via voting or legislation is largely futile since those operating within a vile government cannot understand how terrible it is. He calls on people to reject the government by avoiding any interactions with it, just as he did by not paying taxes, which caused him to be jailed.

Themes, Motifs, and Symbols: rejection of government, individual conscience, unjust laws

Literary Context

Context refers to both the historical and cultural time a text was written. The critical emphasis on context is based on the theory of **situated cognition**, which suggests that human activity is socially situated and unavoidably influenced by its social and cultural surroundings. Therefore, the choices humans make—including those that authors make about their work—must be understood in light of the circumstances that frame them. To truly understand a text, students must be aware of the social and cultural components that influenced the author.

Cultural context refers to the literary, artistic, and musical movements that were going on at the time a work was written. *Civil Disobedience* (Henry David Thoreau) exemplifies the point that an author's purposes are culturally responsive to some degree.

Thoreau, a Romantic Transcendentalist, was influenced by Ralph Waldo Emerson's idea of self-reliance. He was profoundly disturbed by the concepts of majority rule and mandatory conformity to unjust laws; thus, his purpose in writing *Civil Disobedience* was to persuade his readers to be self-reliant by following their own sense of right and wrong, even when that meant disregarding the law.

Historical context refers to the time during which the author was writing. Students must be able to distinguish historical context from the setting of the story itself.

For example, the setting of *The Scarlet Letter* (Nathanial Hawthorne) is seventeenth-century Boston, a Puritan village of the Massachusetts Bay Colony in which conformity is expected as a way of preventing sin. To truly understand the author's work, however, students must know that Hawthorne actually wrote his novel in 1849. Like Thoreau, he was reacting to the ideas of Emerson and the

---

IMPORTANT WORKS

The Scarlet Letter
Author: Nathaniel Hawthorne
Publication Date: 1850
Summary: Hester Prynne is a young mother living in a puritanical New England village who is forced to wear a red A on her clothing to reveal her adultery to the public. Her husband, who she believed was dead, comes to the village in disguise and with a new name— Roger Chillingworth—to meddle in its affairs. Hester refuses to name the father of her child, Pearl, despite the villagers' pressures to do so. Chillingworth discovers that Arthur Dimmesdale, a young minister and the village leader, is the father and confronts him. Unable to handle his guilt, Dimmesdale becomes ill and reveals his paternity before dying. Having lost her love, Hester moves to Europe with Pearl but eventually returns to New England. Upon her death, she is buried next to Dimmesdale.
Themes, Motifs, and Symbols: conformity, guilt, judgment and lack of belonging (the letter A itself), revenge

Romantic Transcendentalists and was interested in the early Women's Rights Movement, which asserted that women can be self-reliant, must have individual rights, and must not conform to practices that subjugated them.

Unlike Thoreau, Hawthorne was a Romantic *Anti*-Transcendentalist: he recognized the human capacity for individuality but also its capacity for darkness, sin, and evil. Hawthorne created a story that explores the admirable but lonely lifestyle of self-reliance, nonconformity, and individualism.

In planning reading instruction, teachers can implement a few context-related best practices in order to ensure students are getting as much as they can from their studies:

Effective teachers frame the study of a literary work with information about its context. They may incorporate a number of different techniques for teaching context:

- They may begin a context-based lesson by having students activate prior knowledge through revisiting previous English or history lessons that might contribute to their understanding of the text.

- If time permits, teachers might assign a short research activity about the historical, cultural, and geographical context of a literary text to help students form the habit of making their own inquiries about background information.

- Alternatively, if pressed for time, the didactic approach of giving a short lecture on the context of a text can also be time well spent.

Teachers may integrate some essential or life question that would make the study of the text more personally meaningful to students.

- Example: If the text is *Civil Disobedience,* an essential question of the unit of study could be, *"When is nonconformity the right alternative?"*

- Teachers may also include additional content-related guiding questions related to context, such as, *"How were the author's artistic choices influenced by the cultural-historical issues of the time period?"; "How are the characters responding to and forming relationships within the social situation of the text?"; "How does this reflect the author's perspective on society?"*

Finally, teachers will return to discussions of context as their studies with the class progress: students look for familiar historical or cultural ideas as well as any intertextual references that may help them gain a deeper understanding of the work.

PRACTICE QUESTION

Question 6 refers to the first stanza of "The Sun Rising" by John Donne, 1572 – 1631.

> *Busy old fool, unruly Sun,*
>
> *Why dost thou thus,*
>
> *Through windows, and through curtains call on us?*
>
> *Must to thy motions lovers' seasons run?*
>
> *Saucy pedantic wretch, go chide*
>
> *Late school-boys and sour prentices,*
>
> *Go tell court-huntsmen that the king will ride,*
>
> *Call country ants to harvest offices,*
>
> *Love, all alike, no season knows nor clime,*
>
> *Nor hours, days, months, which are the rags of time.*

6) **What can the reader infer from knowing that "The Sun Rising" is a metaphysical poem?**

   A. The poem is about philosophical questions.

   B. The poem is using literal language to address questions about human nature.

   C. The poem reflects the concerns of twentieth-century society.

   D. The poem is mocking religion and faith.

LITERARY GENRES

Literature can be classified into **genres** and **subgenres**, categories of works that are similar in format, content, tone, or length.

Most works fall into one of four broad genres:

- nonfiction
- fiction
- drama
- poetry

As students experience each genre, they should receive instruction that integrates all aspects of literacy. That is, students should experience not only reading practice in the genre, but also receive plentiful writing practice and numerous discussion opportunities to deepen their knowledge of the genre they are studying.

DID YOU KNOW?

Bloom's taxonomy is a framework for understanding how humans learn. The first level of the taxonomy is **remembering.** Once they have mastered basic recall, students can be pushed toward **understanding** and applying new information and eventually to **analyzing, evaluating,** and **creating** texts using their knowledge.

Objectives for lessons in genre studies should integrate all levels of Bloom's taxonomy with the goal of equipping students with the ability to understand, interpret, discuss, and create works in various genres.

NONFICTION

Nonfiction is a genre of prose writing that uses information that is true and accurate to the best of the author's knowledge. This quality, however, does not mean that nonfiction is dry or uninspiring; in fact, nonfiction writing comes in many forms, most of which lend themselves to a degree of creativity and originality in terms of how the factual information is presented. For example, **literary nonfiction**, or **creative nonfiction**, is a mix of expressive and informative writing that tells a true, verifiable, or documented story in a compelling, artistic way.

Nonfiction texts are written to inform, reflect, and entertain and may take any of the following forms:

- **essay:** a short work about a particular topic or idea
- **speech:** a short work with a specific purpose, intended to be presented orally in front of an audience
- **news article:** a short recounting of a particular story
- **biography:** a detailed, creative, textual representation of another person's life
- **autobiography:** an account of an individual's life, told by the individual.

Students should be given opportunities to respond to nonfiction texts both in writing (a research report, for example) and with interactive activities (debates and discussions, for example).

When working with nonfiction texts, students should pay particular attention to voice and tone, text structures, and thoughts and ideas. Through guided readings, group discussions, and independent reflection, students should discover that these elements, when taken together with context, can reveal the author's purpose. In successful classrooms the author's purpose is a guiding question, where the study of nonfiction is partly dedicated to helping students recognize and understand bias in literature.

Direct instruction should include the following:

- identifying the rhetorical strategies used in a nonfiction text
- summarizing a nonfiction text by stating the format, the author's purpose, the intended audience, and the central idea or argument
- evaluating the writer's assumptions, claims, appeals, and evidence

As students gain familiarity with the nonfiction genre, they should begin writing their own nonfiction pieces, applying their understanding of the author's purpose and using published texts as models for effective voice, tone, and organization.

> **PRACTICE QUESTION**
>
> 7) Comparing a fiction and nonfiction text on the same topic can help students do which of the following?
>
>   A. understand the difference between a biography and an autobiography
>   B. develop skills in identifying logical fallacies
>   C. recognize differences among genres
>   D. modify the expressiveness of their reading based on the audience

Fiction

Fiction is a prose genre made up of narratives whose details are not based in truth but are instead the creation of the author. Fiction is typically written in the form of novels and short stories. It includes many subgenres; subcategories can be found within some of these subgenres.

Table 1.17. The Subgenres of Fiction and Their Subcategories

Subgenre and Description	Subcategories and Their Descriptions
Folklore • A set of beliefs and stories of a particular people that are passed down through generations; includes many forms/subcategories.	• **fables** • short stories intended to teach moral lessons • **fairy tales** • stories that involve magical creatures such as elves and fairies • **myths** • stories, often involving gods or demigods, that attempt to explain certain practices or phenomena • **legends** • unverifiable stories that seem to have a degree of realism about them • **tall tales** • stories that are set in realistic settings but include characters with wildly exaggerated capabilities
Science fiction • Writers tell imaginative stories that are grounded in scientific and technological theories or realities; often explores ideas involving the future of humanity and its relationship with the universe or with technology.	• **dystopian fiction** • explores social, cultural, and political structures in the context of an imagined world or society

Subgenre and Description	Subcategories and Their Descriptions
Horror • intended to impact the reader via the experiences of fear, paranoia, or disgust; often involves paranormal or psychological content	**mysteries and thrillers** • may also arouse fear or paranoia; tend to be fast-paced and outcome-driven; often focus on human behaviors or relationships, not paranormal activity
Realistic fiction • includes stories that are meant to be relatable for readers; possess a degree of verisimilitude, especially in the dialogue between characters	**historical fiction** • relies on realistic settings and characters from an earlier time to tell new stories
Satire • uses critical humor to reveal vice and foolishness in individuals and institutions; aims to improve the individual or institution being ridiculed • employs rhetorical devices such as sarcasm, irony, mockery, exaggeration, understatement, as well as an honest narrative/speaking voice that is dismayed or appalled by the object of the satire • shows a subject to be ludicrous or wrong while simultaneously appealing to the reader's reason and sense of virtue	

In planning and facilitating fiction studies, teachers should place emphasis on important literary elements like plot, character, setting, and figurative language. (See Literary Elements and Figurative Language in the next section of this chapter for a more detailed discussion of these elements.)

To encourage metacognition, teachers should engage students with fiction in a variety of ways:

▶ Effective teachers might have their students record personal responses to a text in a journal.

▶ Students might also be prompted to compare plot development across a few different texts to illustrate the importance of various plot elements.

▶ A speaking and listening activity might require students to present interviews with the characters: one student may interview another (who is acting as one of the characters) and ask about the character's perspectives and motivations.

▶ Teachers should also make time for students to write fiction: a meaningful assignment might parallel a text read in class. For example, if a class reads a story about a character maturing, students can write a narrative about a personal experience that left them more mature.

PRACTICE QUESTION

8) Which of the following best describes a myth?

    A. a story that includes a magical creature who teaches children a lesson
    B. a story that uses humor to reveal vice or foolishness
    C. a story set in a realistic historical time period
    D. a story that attempts to explain a specific worldview or natural phenomena

DRAMA

Drama is expressive writing that tells a story to an audience through the actions and dialogue of characters, which are brought to life by actors who **play** the roles on stage. Dramatic works, called plays, are written in poetic or lyrical verse, or in regular prose. Along with the dialogue between the characters, authors rely on **stage directions** to describe the sets and to give instructions to the actors about what they are to do.

> **HELPFUL HINT**
>
> **Prosody** is the overall liveliness and expressiveness of reading. It includes appropriate pauses and changes in pitch and intonation based on punctuation and the overall meaning of the piece.

In some plays, actors perform long speeches in which the characters explain their thinking about philosophical ideas or social issues. These **monologues** can be directed toward another character. A monologue delivered as if nobody were listening is called a **soliloquy** (as in Shakespeare's famous "To be or not to be" soliloquy from *Hamlet*).

IMPORTANT WORKS

Hamlet
Author: William Shakespeare
Publication Date: 1603
Summary: Prince Hamlet of Denmark is mourning the death of his father, the king. He also ponders how quickly his mother, Gertrude, married Claudius, his father's brother. The king's ghost visits Hamlet, telling him that Claudius poisoned him and that Hamlet must avenge his father's death. To cover up his plans, Hamlet purposely begins to act strangely. This worries Claudius, who hires Hamlet's friends to spy on him. Hamlet eventually becomes suspicious of everyone around him, including his love interest, Ophelia.

To discover if the ghost's message is true, he stages a play in which a man's brother poisons him to marry his wife. Claudius is clearly upset by the play, so Hamlet confronts his mother. Polonius, Ophelia's father, is hiding in the curtains during this confrontation; thinking he is Claudius, Hamlet stabs and kills Polonius.

Claudius banishes Hamlet to England, but he eventually returns to find Ophelia dead. Her brother Laertes challenges Hamlet to a duel; both die. In the fray, Hamlet also stabs and kills Claudius. Gertrude, who accidentally drinks a cup of poison meant for Hamlet, also dies.
Themes, Motifs, and Symbols: madness, doubt, betrayal, revenge

Sometimes characters in drama (or fiction) have very unique attributes such as a manner of speech, dress, or a catchphrase. Such devices make characters memorable to readers and are known as **character tags**.

Using drama in the classroom is a great way to get students interested in different types of texts. Building on students' innate curiosity and imagination, the possibilities are endless. Acting out dramas helps students work on expressive reading (prosody) and reinforces social and emotional learning as students analyze the emotions and actions of characters.

It is important to have older students think about how both the stage directions and the dialogue contribute to a play's meaning. To jog student interest, especially in linguistically complex dramas like those of Shakespeare, teachers might have students watch video clips of actual performances. Comparing specific scenes performed by different actors stimulates interest and can be used to discuss the different ways a scene can be interpreted.

Students may also benefit from acting out scenes or giving speeches, which allows them to express their own interpretations of the characters or action. To engage students in writing activities, a teacher may prompt them to write their own scripts or a research report on the play's context, author, characters, or subject matter.

PRACTICE QUESTION

9) Drama is a genre well suited for helping students understand
    A. literary context.
    B. prosody.
    C. figurative language.
    D. concepts of print.

POETRY

Poetry is imaginative, expressive verse writing characterized by rhythm, unified and concentrated thought, concrete images, specialized language, and the use of patterns:

- A **line** is a unit of poetry and can be separated by some sort of punctuation, meter, and/or rhyme.
  - Although a line may be a unit of attention, it is usually not a unit of meaning.
- A **stanza** is a group of lines followed by a space.
  - Each stanza may have a specific number of lines; the lines are sometimes arranged in a pattern created by meter and/or a rhyme scheme.

- The pattern is often repeated in each stanza of the poem, although the pattern can be varied for effect.
- A stanza with two lines is a couplet; three lines, a tercet; four lines, a quatrain; five lines, a cinquain; and so on.
- Modern poems may have stanzas with varying lengths or none at all.

Different poetic forms utilize techniques and structures in unique ways.

A **ballad** is a short narrative song about an event that is considered important; they are intended to be recited. Ballads are characterized by a dramatic immediacy, focusing on one crucial situation or action that often leads to a catastrophe. They are frequently about courage, love, political disputes, or military battles.

IMPORTANT WORKS

"The Rime of the Ancient Mariner"
Author: Samuel Taylor Coleridge
Publication Date: 1798
Summary: An old mariner tells a story of his youth to a man traveling to a wedding. The mariner's ship was stuck in ice when an albatross, believed to be good luck, visited. The bird follows the ship after it becomes unstuck. Things start to go wrong after the mariner shoots and kills the bird: there is no wind, no water to drink, and the crew begins to experience nightmares. As penance, they hang the dead bird around the neck of the mariner. The crew members then see a ship in the distance and hope it is their savior, but it is only a ghost ship that brings more bad fortune. Everyone on the ship—except the mariner—drops dead. The mariner remains on the ship with the corpses for seven days but is unable to pray for forgiveness. Eventually, moved by the beauty of the sea creatures, he is able to pray, and the dead albatross suddenly drops from his neck. Although he is rescued, he must atone for his slaughter of the albatross by telling his story as he wanders the world.
Themes, Motifs, and Symbols: nature, dreams, prayer, good versus evil, the albatross as a symbol of sin

The narrator in a ballad tends to be the public voice, speaking without personal judgment until it is interrupted by dialogue. Often, repetition is used to express emotion and reinforce the facts. Though the language of folk ballads is plain—usually without descriptive and figurative qualities—the emotional effect of the forceful language is nevertheless impactful. Literary ballads, like "The Rime of the Ancient Mariner" by Samuel Taylor Coleridge, are distinguished by rhythmic, poetic language and stanzas.

A **sonnet** is a lyrical poem composed of fourteen lines, usually written in iambic pentameter. (For more information on iambic pentameter and meter, see section "Poetic Devices and Structure.") There are two main structural patterns that sonnets follow:

1. The Italian, or Petrarchan, pattern has eight lines (an **octave**) that follow an *abba abba* rhyme scheme, followed by six lines (a **seste**) that follow either a *cde cde* or a *cd cd cd* rhyme scheme.
   - ▷ Usually, the octave in an Italian sonnet poses a question, describes a problem, or tells a story; the seste, then, answers the question, solves the problem, or comments on the story.

2. The English, or Shakespearean, pattern has three groups of four lines (called **quatrains**) and ends with a rhyming **couplet**.
   - ▷ The rhyme scheme of the English sonnet is *abab cdcd efef gg*.
   - ▷ The quatrains present variations on a single theme; the couplet is a concluding remark.

A **haiku** is a short poem format, created in Japan, that consists of three lines and seventeen syllables divided into five, seven, and five syllables on the three lines, respectively.

Finally, a **villanelle** is usually nineteen lines long, containing five stanzas, each with three lines, and a final stanza of four lines. It also includes a refrain—two lines that repeat throughout the poem following a specific pattern. Dylan Thomas's "Do Not Go Gentle into That Good Night" is a common example of a villanelle.

When teaching poetry, teachers should incorporate opportunities into their lesson plans that allow students to respond to both the effect the poem had on them personally as well as the aesthetics of the poem itself.

To introduce poetry and build interest for a poetry unit, an effective teacher might select an especially forceful poem, read it dramatically, and invite students to share their responses in a discussion forum.

When having students analyze poetry, it is best to promote multiple readings, model with a think-aloud of an analytical reading, provide copies of poems that students can annotate, and perhaps establish a process to follow for the collaborative and independent reading of poems. Steps of the process might include

- ▶ an initial reading to experience the mood of the poem and the musicality of the language;

- ▶ a second reading to delineate the pauses and thought units and to identify the speaker;

- ▶ a third close reading to take marginal notes on the structure of the poem, the denotation and connotations of unfamiliar words, the impact of imagery and figurative language, and the meaning of confusing lines or phrases;

- ▶ a final reading to formulate some thematic ideas, drawn from the details.

In conjunction with analyzing poems, students should have opportunity to present their original poetry in classroom "coffee houses." Depending on the literature course, students might also be taught the different poetic forms, like sonnets and ballads, in addition to the characteristics of the different types of poetry, including metaphysical or Romantic.

PRACTICE QUESTION

Question 10 refers to the poem "The Harlem Dancer" by Claude McKay, seen below in its original format:

Applauding youths laughed with young prostitutes

And watched her perfect, half-clothed body sway;

Her voice was like the sound of blended flutes

Blown by black players upon a picnic day.

She sang and danced on gracefully and calm,

The light gauze hanging loose about her form;

To me she seemed a proudly swaying palm

Grown lovelier for passing through a storm.

Upon her swarthy neck black, shiny curls

Luxuriant fell; and, tossing coins in praise,

The wine-flushed, bold-eyed boys, and even the girls,

Devoured her with their eager, passionate gaze;

But, looking at her falsely-smiling face,

I knew her self was not in that strange place.

10) What kind of poem is "The Harlem Dancer"?
    A. a ballad
    B. a villanelle
    C. a sonnet
    D. a satire

LITERARY ELEMENTS

Just as visual artists have the tools of color and shape to communicate ideas, so have writers their literary tools. These tools include point of view, plot, setting, character, tone, and figurative language. Each of these elements contributes to the overall idea that is developed in the text and, as such, can provide valuable insight into the theme of the work.

Setting and Character Development

Setting is the time and place of events in a story. When considering setting, students should look at

- how characters interact with their surroundings;
- how they are influenced by the societal expectations of that time and place;
- how the location and time period impact the development of the story.

Since students could have difficulty understanding the difference between setting and plot, teachers can ask, "How would this story change if it were set in a different time or place?" to help students understand setting.

An author uses **character development** to create characters that are complex and, to some degree, believable. Authors might develop their characters directly by telling the reader explicitly what the character is like by describing traits and values. Sometimes, authors include the thoughts and feelings of the characters themselves, offering readers even more insight.

Authors also develop their characters indirectly by revealing their actions and interactions with others. They might do this by including what one character says or thinks about another and allowing readers to draw their own conclusions. Most authors combine direct and indirect characterization, which ensures that readers know what they need to know and provides opportunities for reflection and interpretation.

PRACTICE QUESTION

11) A reading specialist suggests that the eighth-grade English teacher should invite a guest speaker to present a lecture on the historical background and setting of *Johnny Tremain* before the class reads a portion of the text. Which is the MOST appropriate strategy to use with the guest speaker?

    A. listen-read-discuss
    B. predict-o-gram
    C. peer tutoring
    D. reader's theater

Tone and Mood

The tone of a literary work is created by the author's attitude toward both the reader and the subject of the text. In a sense, it is the tone of voice the author uses to speak to the reader.

Depending on word choice, an author's tone can range from playful, familiar, or sincere to detached, sarcastic, or indifferent. It can be alarmed and forceful or philosophical and serious. It might be concerned or careless, saddened or overjoyed, triumphant or defeated.

Whatever the case, students should be encouraged to consider how the author uses language to convey tone by thinking about what the author is suggesting through language choice. This process will reveal the author's attitude and, ultimately, the theme of the work.

Students should also be able to distinguish the author's tone from **mood**, which is the emotional atmosphere of a literary work that shapes the reader's experience with the text.

Mood is created through an interplay of the literary elements of plot, character, setting, point of view, tone, and figurative language. By examining the emotional effect of the author's choices, readers can further develop their understanding of the text's larger meaning.

PRACTICE QUESTION

12) Which of the following strategies would BEST help a student identify the tone of a literary work?

- A. implementing pre-reading strategies like previewing, scanning, and predicting
- B. using a list-group-label process to dig deeper into key concepts from the work
- C. focusing on the morphology and orthography of words found in the text
- D. identifying specific words in the text that evoke feelings or emotions

POINT OF VIEW

Point of view is the perspective from which the action in a story is told. By carefully selecting a particular point of view, writers are able to control what their readers know. Most literature is written in first-person or third-person point of view:

- In the **first-person** or "I" point of view, the action is narrated by a character within the story.
  - This can make the story feel more believable and authentic to the reader.
  - The reader's knowledge and understanding, however, are limited to what the narrator notices and influenced by what the narrator thinks and values.

A **third-person** point of view is a voice outside the action of the story, what an observer knows, sees, and hears and shares with the reader. A third-person narrator might be

- **omniscient** (able to see into the minds of the characters and share what they are thinking and feeling);

- **partially omniscient** (able to see into the minds of just one or a few characters);
- **limited** (unable to see into the minds of any of the characters and only able to share what can be seen and heard).

The **second-person** point of view uses "you" and can be read as the narrator speaking directly to the reader. It is used mainly in nonfiction texts, particularly in introductory and concluding paragraphs in which the writer might make a direct appeal to the reader to reflect on the points about to be made or already made.

PRACTICE QUESTION

13) Which passage below from "A Mystery of Heroism" by Stephen Crane best exemplifies the third-person omniscient point of view?

   A. "In the midst of it all Smith and Ferguson, two privates of A Company, were engaged in a heated discussion, which involved the greatest questions of the national existence."

   B. "An officer screamed out an order so violently that his voice broke and ended the sentence in a falsetto shriek."

   C. "The officer's face was grimy and perspiring, and his uniform was tousled as if he had been in direct grapple with an enemy. He smiled grimly when the men stared at him."

   D. "No, it could not be true. He was not a hero. Heroes had no shames in their lives, and, as for him, he remembered borrowing fifteen dollars from a friend and promising to pay it back the next day, and then avoiding that friend for ten months."

PLOT

Plot structure is the way the author arranges the events of a narrative. In a conventional plot line, the story is structured around a **central conflict**—a struggle between two opposing forces.

Conflicts in literature can be categorized in general terms as either internal or external, though most stories have a combination of both.

Internal conflicts take place inside the mind of the main character, who might be making a difficult decision, struggling with change, or sorting out priorities. **External conflicts**, on the other hand, occur when a character is in conflict with something or someone in the external world—the elements of nature, another character, supernatural forces, destiny, or society.

A traditional plot structure is usually organized as follows:

- The author begins by introducing the **exposition**, important background information about the setting, the characters, and the current state of the world.

- An **inciting incident** then introduces the antagonist and establishes the conflict.

- As the story progresses, the conflict becomes more complicated and tension increases, moving the story toward a **climax**, or turning point, in which the conflict reaches a crisis point.

- Finally, there is a **resolution** to the conflict, followed by **falling actions**—events that move the characters away from the conflict and into a new life.

To facilitate deep comprehension of literary texts, teachers can help students understand key elements through a **plot diagram**.

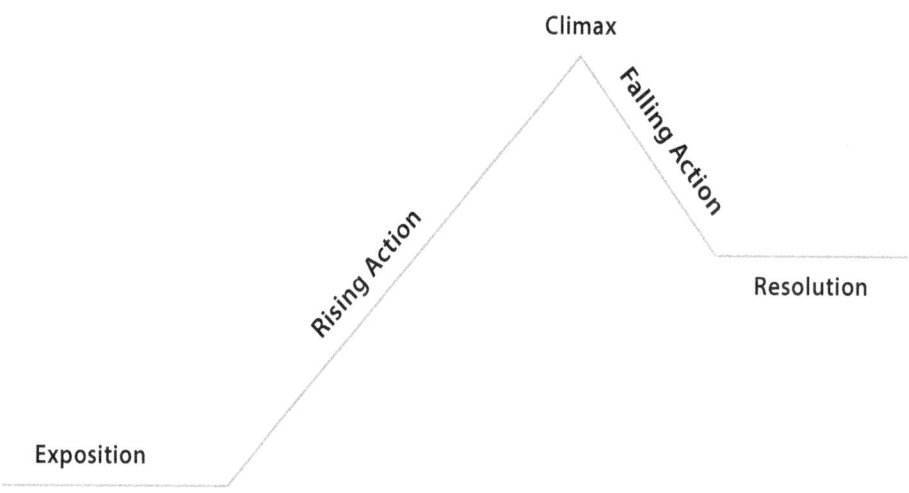

Figure 1.1. Plot Diagram

In studying plot, students should be encouraged to focus on cause-and-effect relationships between events in the story, the conflict, and its resolution. By analyzing how the author chooses to resolve the conflict, the reader can gain a better understanding of the story's theme.

PRACTICE QUESTION

14) Which of the following describes an internal conflict?
    A. In Jack London's "To Build a Fire," the protagonist tries to survive the freezing weather of the Yukon.
    B. In Virginia Woolf's *Mrs. Dalloway*, Clarissa Dalloway questions her choice of husband as she prepares for a party.
    C. In Margaret Atwood's *The Handmaid's Tale*, a group of women try to escape a dystopian society in which they have been enslaved.
    D. In Shakespeare's *Romeo and Juliet*, two lovers try to marry despite the objections of their families.

FIGURATIVE LANGUAGE

Figures of speech are expressions that are understood to have a nonliteral meaning. Rather than stating their ideas directly, authors use figurative language to suggest meaning by speaking of a subject as if it were something else. For example, when Shakespeare says, "All the world's a stage, / And all men and women merely players," he is speaking of the world as if it is a stage. Since the world is not *literally* a stage, the reader has to ask how the two are similar and what Shakespeare might be implying about the world through this comparison. Figures of speech extend the meaning of words by engaging the reader's imagination and adding emphasis to different aspects of their subject.

A **metaphor** is a type of figurative language that describes something that may be unfamiliar to the reader (the topic) by referring to it as though it were something else that is more familiar to the reader (the vehicle). A metaphor stands in as a synonym, interchangeable with its corresponding topic. As readers reflect on the similarities between the topic and the vehicle, they form a clearer understanding of the topic. For example:

- In Shakespeare's *Romeo and Juliet,* Romeo says that "Juliet is the sun."
- By making this comparison, Romeo is comparing Juliet's energy to the brightness of the sun, which is familiar to readers.

IMPORTANT WORKS

Romeo and Juliet
Author: William Shakespeare
Publication Date: 1597
Summary: Juliet, a member of the Capulet family, is engaged to Count Paris per her father's wish. However, she falls in love with Romeo, a member of the Montague family, with whom her family has a longstanding and sometimes violent feud. The two marry in secret, knowing their love will not be permitted by their families. Juliet's cousin Tybalt confronts Romeo about his affections for Juliet; a fight breaks out, and Tybalt kills Romeo's best friend, Mercutio. After killing Tybalt in retribution, Romeo is banished from the city of Verona. Now scheduled to marry Count Paris, Juliet obtains a potion to make her seem dead and devises a plan for Romeo to rescue her. However, a letter explaining the plan never reaches Romeo, and he believes that Juliet actually died. In Juliet's burial crypt, Romeo poisons himself, thinking he has lost his only love. Juliet awakens, finds Romeo dead, and commits suicide.
Themes, Motifs, and Symbols: star-crossed love, fate, role of family, youth and foolishness

A **simile** is a type of figurative language that directly points to similarities between two things. As with a metaphor, the author uses a familiar vehicle to express an idea about a less familiar topic. Unlike a metaphor, however, a simile does not replace the object with a figurative description; it compares the vehicle and topic using *like*, *as*, or similar words. For example:

- In his poem "The Rime of the Ancient Mariner," Coleridge describes his ship as "idle as a painted ship/ Upon a painted ocean."

- He speaks about the boat as if it were painted (unlike Romeo above, who says explicitly that Juliet is the sun itself). The reader understands that paintings do not move, so Coleridge uses this comparison to show the reader that the ship in the poem is completely motionless.

Imagery is vivid description that appeals to the reader's senses of sight, sound, smell, taste, or touch. This type of figurative language allows readers to experience through their senses what is being described. As readers use their imaginations to visualize or recall sensory experiences, they are drawn into the scene of the story or poem.

Hyperbole is an overstatement, or an exaggeration intended to achieve a particular effect. Hyperbole can create humor or add emphasis to a text by drawing the reader's attention to a particular idea. For example:

- A character might say, "I am so hungry, I could eat a horse." Though the character probably will not literally eat a horse, the reader understands that the character is extremely hungry.

Personification is a type of figurative language in which human characteristics are attributed to objects, abstract ideas, natural forces, or animals. For example, writers referring to "murmuring pine trees," are attributing to the pine trees the human ability of murmuring. The writer is using the familiar vehicle of the sound of murmuring to help readers understand the sound pine trees make in the wind.

Symbolism is a literary device in which the author uses a concrete object, action, or character to represent an abstract idea. The significance of the symbol reaches beyond the object's ordinary meaning. As readers notice an author's use of symbolism, they begin to make connections and formulate ideas about what the author is suggesting. Familiar symbols are

- roses representing beauty;
- light representing truth;
- darkness representing evil.

An **allusion**, not to be confused with *illusion*, is a reference to a character or event that is historical, fictional, mythological, or religious, or an artist or artistic work. When readers recognize an allusion, they may make associations that contribute to their understanding of the text. For example:

- If a character is described as having a "Mona Lisa smile," an instant image will arise in the minds of most readers.

▶ Because allusions can be difficult to recognize, especially for young readers whose experiences are limited, teachers must provide instruction in how to recognize, research, and interpret unfamiliar references.

Clichés are common sayings that lack originality but are familiar and relatable to an audience. Though clichés are not necessarily beneficial to the author who is trying to write a wholly original work, they can be helpful for writers who are attempting to show that they can relate to the audience.

Dialect and **slang** are linguistic qualities that authors might incorporate into their writing in order to develop characters or setting. Dialect may reveal where a character is from; slang might be an indication of social, economic, and educational statuses.

> **HELPFUL HINT**
>
> Figures of speech extend the meaning of words by adding emphasis to different aspects of their subject and engaging the reader's imagination.

Authors use **foreshadowing** to hint at events that are going to unfold in a story. Typically, foreshadowing is intended to create a sense of anticipation and suspense in the reader.

Irony comes in different forms. **Verbal irony** is used when a character or narrator says something that is the opposite of what is meant. **Situational irony** occurs when something happens that contradicts what the audience expected to happen. **Dramatic irony** occurs when the audience knows about something of which a character or characters are not aware.

PRACTICE QUESTION

Question 15 refers to the poem "I'm Nobody! Who are you?" by Emily Dickinson.

I'm nobody! Who are you?

Are you nobody, too?

Then there's a pair of us—don't tell!

They'd banish us, you know.

How dreary to be somebody!

How public, like a frog!

To tell your name the livelong day

To an admiring bog!

15) What kind of figurative language is NOT used in the poem?
    A. simile
    B. personification
    C. hyperbole
    D. metaphor

Word Choice

Authors consider a number of factors when selecting words:

- **Denotation** is a word's meaning according to a dictionary.

- **Connotation** is a word's suggested or implied meaning and can be positive or negative, based on emotional associations with the word.

Writers choose words based on how effectively they convey the feelings, ideas, and associations they want to express; when it comes to word choice, precision is of the utmost importance.

For example, Dr. Martin Luther King Jr. said, "I have a dream"; he didn't say "I have a plan."

> **DID YOU KNOW?**
>
> Mark Twain once said, "The difference between the *almost-right* word and the *right* word is really a large matter—it's the difference between the lightning bug and the lightning."

The word *plan* suggests something practical and quotidian, while the word *dream* communicates a much larger desire, a more abstract idea, and a greater vision.

An author might also consider whether to write explicitly or implicitly about a subject based on the degree to which the writer wants the reader to think independently about the subject:

- **Explicit** language is clear, detailed, and exact; the wording is designed to prevent confusion and ambiguity.

- **Implicit** language allows for implied meanings; readers are left to draw their own conclusions.

If writers intend only to inform the reader, they may choose explicit language so that the reader can clearly understand the information being presented.

On the other hand, if writers hope to change readers' behavior, they might use implicit language with the goal of leading readers to their own conclusions.

> **PRACTICE QUESTION**
>
> *The following questions refer to the excerpt from the poem "Ode to the West Wind," by Percy Bysshe Shelley.*
>
> *O wild West Wind, thou breath of Autumn's being,*
>
> *Thou, from whose unseen presence the leaves dead*
>
> *Are driven, like ghosts from an enchanter fleeing,*
>
> *Yellow, and black, and pale, and hectic red,*

Pestilence-stricken multitudes:

O thou, Who chariotest to their dark wintry bed

The wingèd seeds, where they lie cold and low,

Each like a corpse within its grave, until

Thine azure sister of the Spring shall blow

Her clarion o'er the dreaming earth, and fill

(Driving sweet buds like flocks to feed in air)

With living hues and odours plain and hill:

Wild Spirit, which art moving everywhere;

Destroyer and Preserver; hear, O hear!

16) **What is the connotation of the word *Pestilence-stricken* in the poem?**
   A. carrying a contagious disease
   B. full of color
   C. pathetic and sorrowful
   D. dead and decaying

Poetic Devices and Structure

Poets employ poetic devices to create aesthetic effects that impact readers and emphasize meaning. Most poetic devices—including rhyme, rhythm, meter, and repetition—create sound effects or provide structure in a poem.

Table 1.18. Poetic Devices

Device Name	Description
Rhyme scheme	- the arrangement of rhyming words in a stanza or poem
- usually appears at the end of a line but possible for internal rhymes to be part of the scheme
- A frequently used rhyme scheme is present in quatrains, in which the first and third lines rhyme and the second and fourth lines rhyme, creating an *abab* pattern.
- The repeating pattern of sound creates a sense of balance and musicality.
- It produces an aesthetic effect that allows readers to predict the upcoming sounds, thereby freeing them to focus on the ideas.

continued on next page

Table 1.18. Poetic Devices (continued)

Device Name	Description
Slant rhyme	• not considered true rhyme • The poet substitutes assonance or consonance (defined below) for real rhyme.
Internal rhyme	• rhyming two or more words in the same line of poetry
Rhythm	• the drumbeat or heartbeat of a poem • the pattern of accentuated sounds, which creates or heightens the emotional effect of the language
Meter	• an established rhythm within a poem, in which accentuated syllables are repetitive and predictable • Each unit of the meter, called a foot, has stressed and unstressed syllables. • often named by the type and number of feet in one line
Iamb	• a familiar poetic foot • occurs when an unaccented syllable is followed by an accented one, as in the word contain (con-TAIN)
Blank verse	• unrhymed poetry written in iambic pentameter • Many English dramas, including Shakespeare's plays and Milton's *Paradise Lost* are written in blank verse.
Free verse	• poetry without rhyme patterns or regular meter; unpredictable rhythms found in the poem
Repetition	• used to emphasize important ideas and heighten the emotional effect of language • can be of words themselves—a particularly important or charged word might be repeated to draw the reader's attention to it • can sometimes be found only in sounds, as when poets employ assonance or consonance

Assonance	• the inclusion of words with the same vowel sounds within one or two lines of poetry
	• From "Stopping by Woods on a Snowy Evening" (Robert Frost):
	  ◦ "The only other sound's the sweep/ Of easy wind and downy flake"
	  ◦ Here, assonance lends a musicality to the language in a poem.

Device Name	Description
Consonance	- repetition of the same consonant sounds at the end of a stressed syllable but following different vowel sounds in words that are fairly close together.
- From "Stopping by Woods on a Snowy Evening" (Robert Frost):
- "Whose woods these are I think I know."
- Here, the poet uses consonance to highlight particular words; like the other sound devices, it creates a pleasing lyrical effect.

In his poem "A Noiseless Patient Spider," Walt Whitman's speaker reveals the yearning of his soul using a combination of diction, repetition, and consonance.

The repetition of the word *filament* emphasizes the amount of thread that is coming from the spider's body. The use of the words *tirelessly* and *ceaselessly* highlight the similarity between the spider's ongoing efforts to spin her web and the speaker's ongoing effort to connect with the external world.

The six present progressive verbs—the repetition of the - sound—enhance the reader's sense of the relentless efforts on the parts of the spider and the speaker to improve their situations.

> **HELPFUL HINT**
>
> A line with five iambs (ten syllables, beginning with an unstressed syllable and alternating for the rest of the line) is written in iambic pentameter. Shakespeare's verse is mostly written in this meter. From *Romeo and Juliet*, "But, soft! what light through yonder window breaks?" or "But, SOFT! what LIGHT through YONder WINdow BREAKS?"

IMPORTANT WORKS

"Stopping by Woods on a Snowy Evening"
Author: Robert Frost
Publication Date: 1923
Summary: The speaker is driving a horse and carriage on a dark, snowy evening and stops to ponder the woods, which are owned by a villager who will not see the speaker stopping there. The speaker describes the actions of the horse, who shakes its harness, causing the bells on it to chime and perhaps signaling that stopping in such a remote area seems odd. The speaker describes the landscape and the evening itself—dark but lovely on the longest night of the year. The poem ends with the assertion that, though the time spent appreciating the woods and the evening is nice, the driver's journey must continue.
Themes, Motifs, and Symbols: nature, duty, choice, human isolation

"A Noiseless Patient Spider"
A noiseless patient spider,
I mark'd where on a little promontory it stood isolated,
Mark'd how to explore the vacant vast surrounding,
It launch'd forth filament, filament, filament, out of itself,
Ever unreeling them, ever tirelessly speeding them.
And you O my soul where you stand,
Surrounded, detached, in measureless oceans of space,
Ceaselessly musing, venturing, throwing, seeking the spheres to connect them,
Till the bridge you will need be form'd, till the ductile anchor hold,
Till the gossamer thread you fling catch somewhere, O my soul.

While some poets rely on established structures to organize their work, others prefer to create their own rules.

Closed form poetry follows a given form or shape; poems usually have a specified number of lines and a designated number of feet in each line. This poetry also follows a consistent rhyme and meter. Examples of closed forms include blank verse, couplets, the villanelle, the quatrain, the sonnet, and the ballad.

Open form poetry does not have restrictions and allows the poet to create unique arrangements of words and lines that flow naturally or communicate a particular feeling. Often, they use the lengths of the lines to emphasize ideas.

Poets design their poems according to the ideas they are communicating and the mood they hope to convey. Today, poets can choose any form they wish—open or closed.

Some past and present poets chose to reinforce their ideas using **pattern poems**. For example, in the seventeenth century, George Herbert wrote "Easter Wings." The first stanza follows:

Lord, who createdst man in wealth and store,
Though foolishly he lost the same,
Decaying more and more,
Till he became
Most poore:
With thee
O let me rise
As larks, harmoniously,
And sing this day thy victories:
Then shall the fall further the flight in me.

In addition to these poetic devices, poets employ many other kinds of figurative language that are common in literature including metaphors, similes, symbols, and analogies.

> ### PRACTICE QUESTION
>
> Question 17 refers to the following stanza from the poem "Fairest of the Rural Maids" by William Cullen Bryant.
>
> The twilight of the trees and rocks
>
> Is in the light shade of thy locks;
>
> Thy step is as the wind, that weaves
>
> Its playful way among the leaves.
>
> 17) **What sound device is used in the lines "The twilight of the trees and rocks/ Is in the light shade of thy locks"?**
>
>   A. internal rhyme
>   B. consonance
>   C. slant rhyme
>   D. simile

THEMES

Literary texts give concrete form to abstract, thematic ideas. Through a process of carefully examining the concrete details of a text, making evidence-based inferences, and thinking broadly about what these things suggest, readers can come to understand the **theme** of a literary work—the universal message that authors hope to communicate through their artistic choices.

> **HELPFUL HINT**
>
> A **theme** is an idea about some aspect of life or human nature.

By tracing themes across time, location, and culture, students of literature can begin to recognize some of the common experiences that define humanity such as love, loss, power, betrayal, growing old, and coming of age.

To guide students through the process of determining a theme, effective teachers begin by providing instruction in how authors craft their ideas using the literary tools of plot, setting, character, figurative language, and point of view.

> **HELPFUL HINT**
>
> Marxist literary theorists examine how the experiences of and relationships between characters are influenced by socioeconomic class.

Through close reading and analysis of author's choice, students then infer what the author could be suggesting about life or human nature.

To direct student attention to the thematic ideas of a text, effective teachers might

- use two-column response journals to have students record interesting or memorable quotes and their reactions to them;

- use focus questions that push students to make connections with the text, *like how did the author's use of _____ affect your reaction to the story? Why would the author want you to react that way? What about this story can you relate to your own life?*;

- facilitate a discussion about the relationship between elements of the text, including the plot and character development, tone, and setting;

- have students record words or images in their journals that are repeated and elements and ideas that are paired or contrasted;

- take the time to not only explain figurative language to students but also provide instruction in the thought processes that make analysis possible;

- explicitly identify signal words or phrases, like *as a result,* and discuss their meaning with students.

By asking students to analyze the author's purpose using specific details, effective teachers push students to make connections, read closely, and improve their critical reading and thinking skills.

PRACTICE QUESTION

18) An ELA teacher is working with a small group of students on identifying theme. Which of the following self-guiding questions should the teacher have students ask themselves?

    A. What did I like best about this story?
    B. Why did I read this story?
    C. What is the author trying to teach me in this story?
    D. How is the author different from others I have read?

Literary Theory

Living in a diverse world makes the ability to recognize and empathize with multiple perspectives imperative. These abilities are also a powerful way to deepen one's understanding of art and literature.

Literary theory is using a set of principles or a system of ideas to interpret literature from a unique angle:

- By viewing a single text through a variety of lenses, readers gain a depth of understanding that far exceeds that which can be developed based on straightforward analysis.

- Teaching literary theory allows instructors to highlight how the assumptions that people make can color their interpretation of literary works and the world as a whole.

Before thinking about a literary text from different theoretical perspectives, students must first have a general understanding of the text; in other words, teachers should engage students in the processes of literary criticism before introducing a particular theoretical framework. Specifically, teachers may have students engage in activities or discussions that prime their thinking to prepare them for the theory that they will be applying.

For example, an effective teacher might prepare students to analyze *The Great Gatsby* via a Marxist approach to criticism by asking them to consider the relationship between financial wealth and social status.

Reader-response theory is centered on the idea that as readers read, they experience a transaction with the text. The feelings and associations readers experience influence their interpretation of what they are reading:

- In the process of constructing meaning, the reader's responses blend with the author's intended meanings so that the reader ends up participating in the creative process.

- This means that there is no single correct interpretation of a text; understanding will be unique to each reader. (All interpretations, however, must still be grounded in text evidence.)

Feminist literary theory involves asking questions about the degree to which a literary text perpetuates the ideas that women are inferior to and dependent on men or that the perspective of a woman is not as interesting or significant as that of a man.

IMPORTANT WORKS

The Great Gatsby
Author: F. Scott Fitzgerald
Publication Date: 1925
Summary: Narrator Nick Carraway moves to Long Island in 1922, where his neighbor is the mysterious, self-made Jay Gatsby. Nick's cousin Daisy is trapped in a marriage with Tom, who is having an affair with a woman named Myrtle. Gatsby eventually invites Nick to one of his lavish parties and asks him to bring Daisy, with whom he had a past relationship. Daisy and Gatsby begin an affair, which enrages Tom. During an argument, Tom reveals that Gatsby's wealth comes from bootlegging, leading Daisy and Gatsby to angrily drive off with Daisy at the wheel. She accidentally hits and kills Myrtle. Myrtle's husband then kills Gatsby, believing he was the one responsible for his wife's death.
Themes, Motifs, and Symbols: social class/social hierarchy, love and marriage, the American dream

One goal of feminist theory is to challenge the view that being female is the opposite of being male, that having characteristics of sensitivity or a desire to nurture others makes an individual "feminine" and weak. A related intention is to free both males and females from the rigid thinking perpetuated by traditional concepts of gender identity.

Feminists maintain that as students are confronted by feminist criticism, they will begin to recognize biases in their own thinking and in popular culture, making them more equipped to evaluate and challenge traditional gender roles.

Closely related to feminist theory is **queer theory**, which investigates texts by asking questions about both gender and sexuality. This lens of analysis involves recognizing and challenging all cultural assumptions related to sex and gender, especially those related to identity.

One pillar of queer theory is that a person is not defined by one's sexuality and cannot be categorized in such terms because one's sexual identity is in a constant state of change. A queer analysis of a literary text challenges assumptions about the rigidity of sexuality and identifies alternative ways of thinking about the characters or their situations.

For example, most commentary on Walt Whitman's poem "Song of Myself" points to Whitman's homosexual imagery; a queer analysis might come to the conclusion that Whitman finds all experiences to be erotic, even the undulating waves of the ocean, and that homosexuality constitutes only one small part of his sexual identity.

Deconstructionist literary criticism focuses on dissecting and uncovering the writer's assumptions about what is true and false, good and bad.

Deconstructionists begin by examining language, which they consider a distortion of reality. They explain that meaning in language comes from differences: people understand *good* as the absence of *bad*; that is, one thing is understood as the absence of its opposite. By traditional thinking, reason or logic is the absence of emotion. By extension, if it is good to be rational, then it is not good to be emotional.

IMPORTANT WORKS

"Song of Myself"
Author: Walt Whitman
Publication Date: 1855 (1881 when republished under this title)
Summary: This poem is an ode to the author's self and an important work in the transcendental movement. Whitman explains that humans have a transcendental understanding of themselves and, along with all other entities on Earth, have a "self" that contains part of the broader universe. Further, the self is united with God, which Whitman calls the "absolute self." Humans, therefore, have a sort of brotherhood with God and all things, as they, too, contain part of the entire universe.
Themes, Motifs, and Symbols: nature, self, identity, spirituality

The goal of deconstructionism is to identify these binaries in language and thinking in order to inspire investigation into possible other alternatives. As deconstructionist critics read a literary text, they examine linguistic contradictions and ambiguities in order to uncover incongruities in the underlying reasoning. Deconstructionists argue that, because of these inconsistencies, no text can be reduced to one correct meaning or interpretation.

Semiotic analysis is the study of signs, signals, visual messages, and gestures. In semiotics, a sign system is a set of behaviors or things which are analyzed as if they are symbols that represent ideas.

In Ernest Hemingway's novel *The Old Man and the Sea*, the sign system of the man's struggle with the fish and his determination to show the boy what a man can do signifies many ideas about human potential. To interpret a message using semiotic analysis, the following must be considered:

- Who created the message?
- For whom was it created?
- What was the context?

Marxist theory focuses on the economic systems that structure society and the ways in which human behavior is motivated by a desire for economic power. According to this theory, life cannot be understood through abstract principles or ideals but instead only in terms of the concrete, actual conditions that people experience.

Formalism or **New Criticism** emphasizes closely reading a text and analyzing how literary elements create meaning in it; it is unconcerned with the text's effect on the reader.

IMPORTANT WORKS

The Old Man and the Sea
Author: Ernest Hemingway
Publication Date: 1952
Summary: Cuban fisherman Santiago has caught nothing in eighty-four days. His helper, Manolin, is forced to work on another boat, though he continues to check on Santiago and talk baseball with him. Santiago goes into the Gulf Stream and hooks a giant marlin. For three days, he struggles with the fish but also appreciates its strength and beauty. He eventually kills the marlin with a harpoon and sails back to shore. Sharks are attracted to the marlin's blood; though Santiago tries to fight them off, they consume all of his catch. He returns with only the marlin's carcass, angry at himself for fishing so far out and killing such a noble creature. Manolin and Santiago are reunited; Manolin agrees to return to Santiago's boat.
Themes, Motifs, and Symbols: friendship, man versus nature, defeat, perseverance

> **PRACTICE QUESTION**

The following questions refer to this excerpt from the poem "In an Artist's Studio" by Christina Rossetti.

One face looks out from all his canvases,

One selfsame figure sits or walks or leans:

We found her hidden just behind those screens,

That mirror gave back all her loveliness.

A queen in opal or in ruby dress,

A nameless girl in freshest summer-greens,

A saint, an angel;–every canvas means

The same one meaning, neither more or less.

19) A critic comments that, in the poem, the famous artist's paintings of the woman suggest that he views her as an object to be admired and not as a real person. This critic asserts that the poem reveals a dangerous and biased assumption—that by portraying women in artistic ways, men are honoring women. The critic argues that, on the contrary, to make a woman the center of a piece of art is to objectify her.

What literary theory does this critic represent?

   A. Marxist
   B. feminist
   C. deconstructionist
   D. reader-response

Building Comprehension of Fiction

Readers of all ages often enjoy fiction texts, thanks to relatable characters and well-developed plots. Teachers often use familiar stories as a springboard to more in-depth comprehension because students are familiar with the literal meaning of the text.

While there are many specific strategies to aid students in their comprehension of literary texts, some of the most common are discussed below.

Graphic or Semantic Organizers

- ▶ storyboards or event sequence frames or timelines
- ▶ story maps (beginning, middle, end) or plot diagrams (rising action, climax, falling action, resolution)
- ▶ character maps (actions, feelings, appearance, dialogue)
- ▶ character trait identification charts

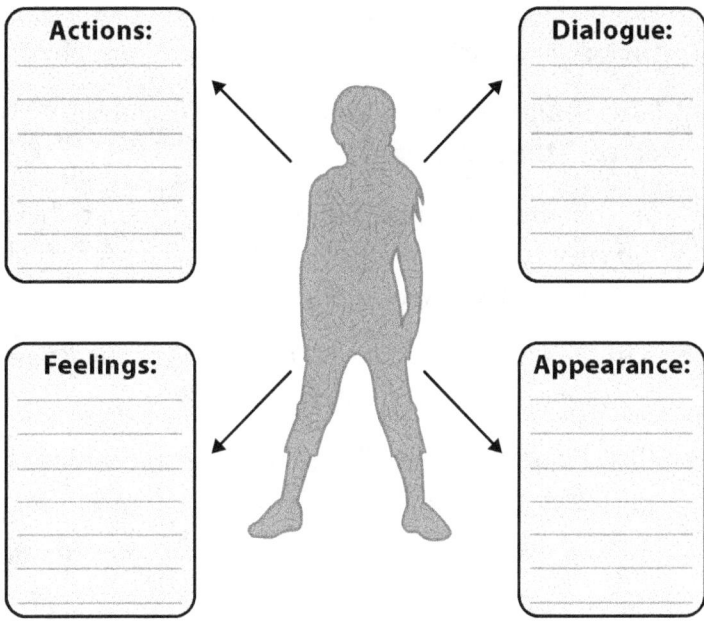

Figure 1.2. Character Map

GUIDED COMPREHENSION QUESTIONS

- those requiring students to underline, highlight, and locate the answer in the text
- those requiring a constructed response
- cloze exercises in which a portion of the text is removed and readers must fill in the blanks

SUMMARIZATION AND MAIN IDEA EXERCISES

- written retellings that ask students to recall and write down important parts of the story in their own words
- exercises that ask students to create an outline of the story
- asking students to identify main or central ideas in the story
- asking students to identify themes or messages within the story

SPECIFIC TARGETED STRATEGIES

- **Directed Reading-Thinking Activity (DR-TA):** Students make predictions and read up to a preselected stopping point; then they evaluate and refine predictions based on text evidence.
- The **QAR Strategy** encourages students to identify the type of question and think about *how* to find the answer.

- ▷ "Right There" questions are literal and require only the location of the relevant part.

- ▷ "Think and Search" questions require synthesis from multiple parts of the text.

- ▷ "Author and You" questions require the text to have been read, but the answer is not directly in the text. They are typically inference and depth of knowledge (DOK) questions.

- ▷ "On My Own" questions require background knowledge and do not directly rely on text evidence.

▶ **The SQ3R strategy** was developed for reading textbooks, but it is useful for many different reading materials.

- ▷ **S**urvey: previewing the text and taking note of graphics, headings, and so forth

- ▷ **Q**uestion: generating questions about the text after previewing

- ▷ **R**ead: reading and looking for answers to the questions

- ▷ **R**ecite: rehearsing or saying the answers to the questions

- ▷ **R**eview: reviewing text and answering or responding to any other questions

▶ **K-W-L Charts** help students think about what they already know and what they want to know before reading as well as what they learned after reading.

- ▷ The K stands for "What I already know" about the topic.

- ▷ The W is "What I want to know."

- ▷ The L is completed after reading to state, "What I learned."

Group or Paired Strategies

▶ **Reciprocal teaching** assigns roles to groups of four students who work together to read and comprehend a text.

▶ **Think-pair-share** pairs students to answer comprehension questions about a text:

- ▷ First, students think about their own answer by activating background knowledge.

- ▷ They then pair with another student or a small group.

▷ Students share their answer with their group or partner and then the entire class.

▶ **Peer-Assisted Learning Strategies (PALS)** require students to partner with a classmate; they then take turns providing each other assistance and feedback in reading comprehension.

PRACTICE QUESTION

20) **Which strategy can be employed to help students activate background knowledge before they read a text?**

   A. reciprocal teaching

   B. peer-assisted learning strategies

   C. plot diagrams

   D. K-W-L Chart

Answer Key

1) **C** — A strong familiarity with the exact details of the text, while valuable, is less important to constructivists than an individual's personal understanding of the text.

2) **B** — In her diary, Mary Chesnut recorded her observations about the Civil War, which took place during the years in which she chronicled her thoughts. The work is also published under the title *A Diary from Dixie*.

3) **A, C** — Charles Dickens and Robert Browning both wrote during the Victorian Period (ca. 1832 – ca. 1901).

4) **B, D, E** — *Things Fall Apart, House of Spirits,* and *The Kite Runner* all explore the effects of colonialism on indigenous populations.

5) **A** — The *Giver* tells the story of a boy in a dystopian society who must decide what to do with the memories he has been given.

6) **A** — Philosophical concerns are often the subject of metaphysical poetry.

7) **C** — Comparing a fiction and nonfiction text on the same topic can help students understand how the genres differ.

8) **D** — A myth is a story, often involving gods or demigods, that attempts to explain a practice, worldview, or natural phenomena.

9) **B** — Drama is particularly useful in helping students develop oral reading skills and prosody.

10) **C** — "The Harlem Dancer" is a sonnet. The poem develops a theme about the dancer, contains fourteen lines (three quatrains with an *abab, cdcd,* and *efef* rhyme scheme), and ends with a rhyming couplet.

11) **A** — In this strategy, students listen to a lecture on a topic, read a text, and then discuss similarities or differences in the lecture versus text.

12) **D** — Identifying specific evocative words will aid students in connecting word choice and tone.

13) **D** — The narrator is reporting the thoughts of the character, as the character's memory about not acting heroic in the past is revealed.

14) **B** — Option B describes an internal conflict in which Mrs. Dalloway struggles within her own mind to understand the meaning of her choices.

15) **D** — There is no metaphor in this poem. The line, "How public, like a frog" is a simile. The frog who can tell his name is personification. The line, "To tell your name the livelong day" is hyperbole.

16) **D** — The fall leaves are described as "leaves dead" and "like ghosts," so the connotations of the phrase *pestilence-stricken multitudes* is that the leaves are dead and decaying.

17) **B** — Consonance is repetition of the same consonant sounds at the end of a stressed syllable. *Twilight* ends with the same sound as *light*.

18) **C** — The theme is the message or lesson that the author is trying to teach.

19) B This argument reflects feminist theory because it discusses popular perceptions of women and evaluates how those perceptions might be detrimental to the fight for gender equality.

20) D The K stands for "What I already know" about the topic. The W is "What I want to know," and the L is completed after reading to state, "What I learned."

Reading Informational Texts

In today's information-rich world, students benefit from having a solid understanding of the goals and structures of informational texts. In fact, it is just as important for students to know the format of a current event article, editorial, or a speech as it is for them to know the structure of a sonnet or a short story. To interpret informational texts, students benefit from making connections between texts; an effective teacher might therefore assign multiple articles on the same subject and ask students to make comparisons.

AUTHOR'S PURPOSE

Nonfiction texts are written to persuade, inform, explain, entertain, or describe. Authors who write to **persuade** try to convince the reader to act or think a certain way. They may use specific reasons and supporting evidence to do this. Persuasive writers also use **rhetoric**, language chosen specifically for its particular effect, to influence readers.

Writing to **inform** is as straightforward as the term suggests: the author sets out simply to communicate information to the reader. Purely informative writing is found in many textbooks and news articles. Some informational writing may also **instruct** the reader; types of this writing include lists, steps to be followed, and information presented in a sequential order. Similar to informing, some writing **explains**. It might define a term, discuss how things are similar or different, or explain a problem and its solution.

Nonfiction may also entertain. Typically, this type of writing will **narrate**, or tell a (true) story. Like fiction, narrative nonfiction (sometimes referred to as literary nonfiction) will include a setting, characters, and a plot. The writer may also use figurative language and other devices to entertain the reader. Finally, nonfiction texts may **describe** something, such as a detailed description of an event, person, place, or even inanimate object.

The acronym **PIEED** helps students think about the author's purpose. Figure 2.1. illustrates each of the PIEED purposes:

- ▸ <u>P</u>ersuade
- ▸ <u>I</u>nform
- ▸ <u>E</u>xplain
- ▸ <u>E</u>ntertain
- ▸ <u>D</u>escribe

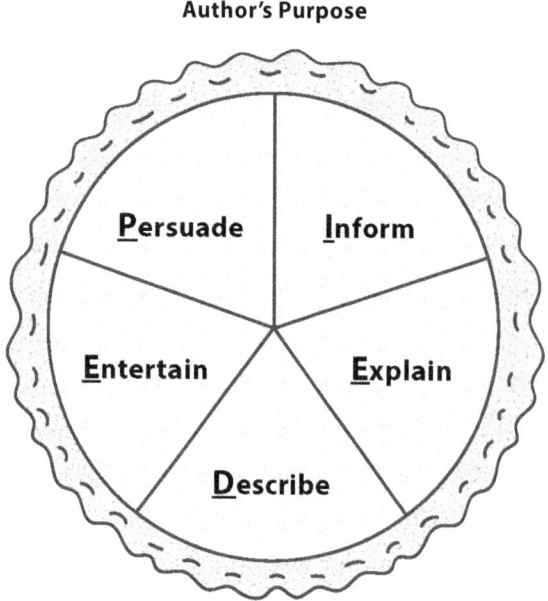

Figure 2.1. PIEED (Author's Purpose)

Nonfiction takes many forms, as described in Table 2.1. The form of a work of nonfiction is often related to the author's purpose. To identify the purpose of a text, many educators use the following step-by-step process:

1. While reading the text, think of the question "Why did the author write this?"
2. After reading, complete the statement "The author wrote this mainly to _____."
3. Find important details in the text that support the statement; if no such details exist, the purpose statement might need to be modified.

Table 2.1. Forms of Nonfiction

Form	Description
Essay	a short work about a particular topic or idea

Form	Description
Speech	a short work with a specific purpose, intended to be presented orally in front of an audience
News article	a short recounting of a particular story
Biography	a detailed, creative textual representation of a person's life
Autobiography	an account of an individual's life, told by the individual

PRACTICE QUESTION

1) A high school teacher is working with students to identify the purpose of a science article in preparation for similar questions on the SAT/ACT. Which advice should he give students to help them answer the question, "What is the author's purpose?"?

   A. ask whether the author achieved her purpose for writing the text
   B. look for specific text evidence that supports an assertion about the author's purpose
   C. tell them that the purpose will generally be revealed explicitly in the introductory paragraph
   D. tell them that a "call to action" never gives possible clues to the author's purpose

> **HELPFUL HINT**
>
> A purpose statement aims to summarize the specific goals or topics of a written work; it is a declarative sentence.

Text Structure

Authors organize nonfiction texts with a structure that suits their purpose. This structure may be a **sequence** of events, such as a news story about the days leading up to an important event. It might also be a thorough **description** of something, as in the opening paragraph of an essay describing a person or place in detail.

Many historical texts use a **cause-and-effect** pattern in which the cause is presented first, and the result is discussed next. A chapter in a social studies text about the Industrial Revolution, for example, might follow this pattern, citing the Industrial Revolution as the cause for a change in working and living conditions in many cities.

Other works are organized in a **problem-solution** structure, in which a problem is presented and then a possible solution is discussed. Teachers might introduce this structure through a collaborative activity in which students identify a problem in the classroom, school, or community. They can then write a letter to a decision-maker about the issue and a possible solution. Finally, students can read other problem-solution texts to see how other authors structure their arguments.

Students can use a **compare and contrast** structure to explain how two things from their everyday experiences are similar and different. Charts and other graphic organizers can help them organize their thoughts and understand this structure. A teacher might ask students, for example, to use a **Venn diagram** to determine the similarities and differences presented in a text.

IMPORTANT WORKS

Nature
Author: Ralph Waldo Emerson
Publication Date: 1836
Summary: Emerson describes the foundational principles of transcendentalism, a philosophical movement that esteems nature and dislikes formal religion. He explains how humans can find solitude in nature, which allows them to experience God free from the constraints of the modern world. He further explains how humans can use nature for societal advancements, such as those of the Industrial Revolution. He elaborates on the true beauty in natural things, the role of language in human existence and the description of the world, and how language can be corrupted. He argues that nature is a path to truth and morality. Linking nature and God, Emerson argues that nature is a way humanity can experience the act of creation. He criticizes strict empiricism as reductionist and instead encourages a focus on the whole of the natural world.
Themes and Rhetorical Strategies: nature, problems with modern society, unity, religion, modern science

It is helpful to integrate reading and writing nonfiction/expository texts that use the same structure. This approach is used in many textbooks and curricular resources based on the Common Core State Standards.

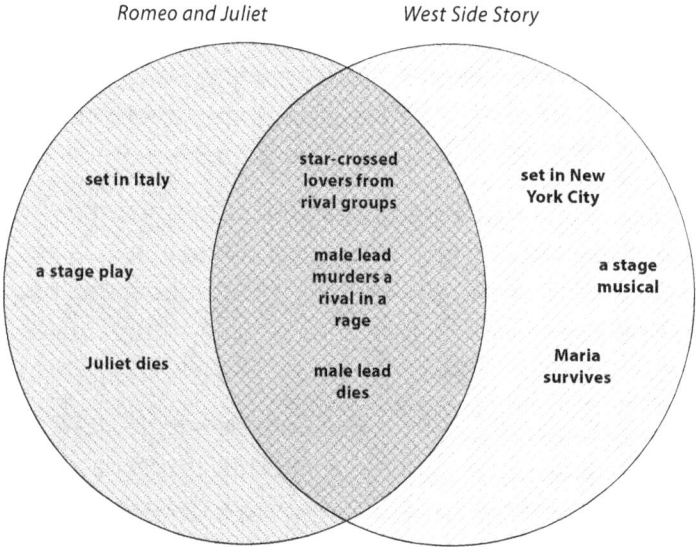

Figure 2.2. Venn Diagram Example

PRACTICE QUESTION

The question below refers to the following excerpt taken from Chapter IV of the essay *Nature* by Ralph Waldo Emerson.

Words are signs of natural facts. The use of natural history is to give us aid in supernatural history: the use of the outer creation, to give us language for the beings and changes of the inward creation. Every word which is used to express a moral or intellectual fact, if traced to its root, is found to be borrowed from some material appearance. *Right* means *straight; wrong* means *twisted. Spirit* primarily means *wind; transgression*, the crossing of a *line; supercilious*, the *raising* of the *eyebrow*. We say the *heart* to express emotion, the *head* to denote thought; and *thought* and *emotion* are words borrowed from sensible things, and now appropriated to spiritual nature. Most of the process by which this transformation is made, is hidden from us in the remote time when language was framed; but the same tendency may be daily observed in children. Children and savages use only nouns or names of things, which they convert into verbs, and apply to analogous mental acts.

2) How does Emerson structure the information in this section of text?
   A. from general to specific
   B. sequentially
   C. chronologically
   D. using spatial details

Identifying Central Ideas

Nonfiction texts contain a **central** or **main idea**. Identifying this idea is an important—though sometimes challenging—skill for students. When being taught to look for the main idea, students should start with simple texts and identify the **topic** of each. For example, the topic of a text might be "horses." Students then ask themselves a question such as, "What is the author saying about horses?" The answer to that question is the central idea of the text. For example, the answer might be "Horses are animals that have helped humans throughout history."

An **implicit main idea**—which is not explicating stated in the text—is more difficult to identify. Students must synthesize information and details from many parts of the text. The following process can help students identify the main idea:

> **HELPFUL HINT**
>
> When stated explicitly, the main idea is referred to as a **thesis**, or thesis statement.

Identify the main idea of each paragraph first. It might be stated explicitly as a topic sentence, or it might be implicit. If the idea is implicit, students will need to summarize the paragraph in a single sentence in their own words.

After determining the main idea of each paragraph, students can think about what these main ideas have in common or make a "summary of summaries."

Students should check their main idea statements to make sure they have no specific details or examples and that they encapsulate only the most important points.

Because identification of the central idea and summarization are similar thought processes, these skills are often taught together. Teachers might also introduce the central idea as the most important idea within the summary.

PRACTICE QUESTION

When a fire destroyed San Francisco's American Indian Center in October of 1969, American Indian groups set their sights on the recently closed island prison of Alcatraz as a site of a new Indian cultural center and school. Ignored by the government, an activist group known as "Indians of All Tribes" sailed to Alcatraz in the early morning hours with eighty-nine men, women, and children. They landed on Alcatraz, claiming it for all the tribes of North America. Their demands were ignored, and so the group continued to occupy the island for the next nineteen months, its numbers swelling up to 600 as others joined. By January of 1970, many of the original protestors had left, and on June 11, 1971, federal marshals forcibly removed the last residents.

3) What is the main idea of this passage?

   A. The government refused to listen to the demands of American Indians.
   B. American Indians occupied Alcatraz in protest of government policy.
   C. Few people joined the occupation of Alcatraz, weakening its effectiveness.
   D. The government took violent action against protestors at Alcatraz.

TEXTUAL EVIDENCE

The goal in courtrooms, science labs, and classrooms is not just to arrive at conclusions, but to come to *evidence-based* conclusions. Within the constructivist framework, students are urged to formulate responses to and interpretations of the texts they read; then, they must cite specific evidence to support their conclusions.

In the early grades, students begin by referring to the text when looking for answers to teacher-provided questions. When they get older, they move to asking their own questions and quoting text to articulate their answers. By middle school, they should be able to cite details in the text in order to explain and justify their thinking.

In addition to using evidence themselves, students must also be able to identify and interpret an author's use of evidence in the context of an informational text. They must then learn how to evaluate arguments based on the evidence and claims made in support of those arguments. Students should learn how to identify **supporting details**—the evidence provided by the author to support the main idea. They can then evaluate the reliability of an article by exploring the effectiveness and suitability of the supporting details provided by the author.

An effective teacher might have students first identify the claims of an article, then look for the evidence the writer includes to substantiate the claim. Evidence can then be evaluated based on its source. Supporting details are often introduced by **signal words** that explain to the reader how one idea is connected to another. Table 2.1. provides a list of some of the most common signal words and their associations.

Table 2.1. Common Signal Words and Their Associations

Association/Reason for Use	Signal Words
Adding information	additionally, also, in addition, furthermore, too
Providing an example	for example, for instance, in other words, in particular
Showing cause and effect	because, so, therefore, consequently
Comparing	in the same way, like, likewise, similarly
Contrasting	alternatively, conversely, instead of, otherwise, unlike
Providing sequence	first, second, next, after, before, then, finally

Students should learn to differentiate between facts and opinions in order to effectively analyze an author's argument:

▸ **Facts** are based in truth and can usually be proven; they are pieces of information that have been confirmed or validated.

▸ **Opinions** are judgments, beliefs, or viewpoints that are not based on evidence and are often stated in descriptive, subjective language that is difficult to define or prove.

Students should be aware that, even in informational texts, they will have to draw their own **inferences** to fully make sense of what they are reading. Readers draw inferences when they use their own knowledge in combination with details from the text to understand the meaning of a sentence, paragraph, or passage.

> **HELPFUL HINT**
>
> While opinions can be included in informative texts, they often offer little impact unless they are supported by some kind of evidence.

> **PRACTICE QUESTION**
>
> *Increasingly, companies are turning to subcontracting services rather than hiring full-time employees. This provides companies with many advantages. For example, subcontractors offer greater flexibility, reduced legal responsibility to employees,*

continued on next page

and a lower possibility of unionization within the company. However, it has also led to increasing confusion and uncertainty over the legal definition of employment. Recently, the courts have grappled with questions about the hiring company's responsibility in maintaining fair labor practices. Companies argue that they delegate that authority to the subcontractors, while unions and other worker advocate groups argue that companies still have a legal obligation to the workers who contribute to their business.

4) According to the passage, which of the following is NOT an advantage of using subcontracting services?

   A. greater flexibility
   B. uncertainty about the legal definition of employment
   C. reduced legal responsibility to employees
   D. lower possibility of unionization within the company

ARGUMENTATION

A written argument begins with a proposition, thesis, or assertion that will be defended throughout the work. A set of assumptions may then be established. Next, research and evidence are presented in an organized way; opposing arguments are often mentioned and countered. In learning to evaluate arguments, students should receive plentiful instruction and practice in critical thinking.

Critical thinking involves asking questions about the quality of reasoning or the validity of beliefs or assumptions. Rather than accepting information as necessarily true, students should be taught to ask questions and formulate responses to arguments presented in any text. Effective teachers provide questions to guide critical thinking:

- What are the conclusions the author is making and what evidence is being provided?
- What assumptions are being made in order for this reasoning to work?
- Is there any fallacious reasoning, deceptive, ambiguous, or omitted information?
- Is the evidence accurate and reliable?
- What other causes or conclusions are possible?

Students must be able to evaluate evidence, identify errors in reasoning, and recognize the rhetorical strategies that are being used in a given piece of informative writing. In evaluating evidence, students should ask questions about its relevancy and its reliability. Evidence **relevancy** depends on how closely the evidence is related to the argument and how recently the information was established:

- Evidence must be representative, meaning that it speaks directly to the situation or claim being discussed.

- Evidence that is irrelevant or too dated should be viewed with a skeptical eye.

- Evidence must also come from a **reliable** source, the definition of which will vary depending on the topic and the kind of evidence that is being gathered.

Part of assessing an argument is understanding its logical construction. With **deductive reasoning,** the argument begins with a general statement or premise that is proven. Then, by applying the premise to a set of circumstances, specific conclusions can be drawn. If the initial premise is not valid, the reasoning is not sound or logical.

With **inductive reasoning,** facts are gathered and conclusions are drawn from these facts. If there are enough facts to prove a conclusion, the conclusion is supported. Reasoning breaks down when there is contradictory or incomplete evidence. A **logical fallacy** is an error or breakdown in logical reasoning. Students should learn to recognize logical fallacies in order to evaluate the effectiveness of evidence in informative texts. Some of the most common logical fallacies are discussed in Table 2.2.

Table 2.2. Common Logical Fallacies

Logical Fallacy	Description
Slippery slope	The main argument is based on the assumption that if one particular thing happens, a series of other specific things will follow.
Hasty generalization	An individual comes to a conclusion without enough evidence, based on prior experiences or assumptions.
Circular argument	The argument is simply restated repeatedly with no inclusion of new evidence.
Red herring	Distracting information is introduced, moving the focus away from the most important points of the argument.
False analogy	This describes an argument based on an incorrect or misleading analogy.
Non sequitur	This is the introduction of an argument that does not logically flow from the preceding arguments.
False dilemma (either/or **fallacy** or dichotomy fallacy)	The argument is constructed so that it appears there are only two possible options to choose from.

continued on next page

Table 2.2. Common Logical Fallacies (continued)

Logical Fallacy	Description
Dichotomous thinking	An argument is set up in dichotomies—pairs of opposing terms (good/evil, true/false)—so that people can only see the extremes of a situation rather than its complexities and subtleties.

PRACTICE QUESTION

5) Which logical fallacy is represented in the argument below?

Why should I care about the corruption on the school board? The property taxes are of far greater concern.

- A. hasty generalization
- B. false analogy
- C. red herring
- D. slippery slope

RHETORICAL STRATEGIES

Rhetoric is the powerful use of language and the purposeful expression of ideas meant to command the reader's attention. In rhetoric, a deliberate effort is made to show the connection between points, to relate each point to the central idea, and to use words that will elicit a response from an audience. In addition to giving careful thought to the words chosen, writers consider how to position words in a sentence in order to make the biggest impact. For example:

- ▶ To emphasize a word, a writer might repeat the word and place it at the end of a sentence.

- ▶ Parallel sentence construction might be used to accentuate the key facets of an issue.

- ▶ Figures of speech may be used to engage the reader's attention and connect new ideas to those that are familiar.

- ▶ A series of vivid images may be included to describe events in more detail.

- ▶ Writers might also include personal anecdotes to illustrate their points.

In a speech to Americans after the assassination of Martin Luther King Jr., Robert Kennedy said:

"We can move in that direction as a country, in greater polarization—Black people amongst Blacks, and White amongst Whites—filled with hatred toward one another. Or we can make an effort, as Martin Luther King did, to understand, and

> to comprehend, and replace that violence, that stain of bloodshed that has spread across our land, with an effort to understand, compassion, and love."

Kennedy uses several rhetorical strategies to convince his audience to change their approach to the issue of race. He contrasts the words *hate* and *hatred* with the words *love* and *compassion*. He uses a vivid image—the "stain of bloodshed"—to describe the approach of the past. To define the concept of polarization, he repeats the word *understand* and creates a parallel between the verbs *understand, comprehend,* and *replace* in order to emphasize his goals for race relations in the United States.

IMPORTANT WORKS

Statement on the Assassination of Martin Luther King, Jr.
Speaker: Robert Kennedy
Date: April 4, 1968
Summary: Kennedy learns of King's assassination after landing in Indianapolis, Indiana, where he planned a campaign stop in a predominantly African American neighborhood in his bid for the Democratic presidential nomination. He realizes that those listening likely had not yet heard of King's assassination. In this impromptu speech, Kennedy explains that there are two paths: one filled with hatred and bitterness and one of compassion and love. He notes that he understands loss—having lost his brother to murder—though his brother was killed by a fellow White man. He calls for White and Black Americans to try to understand each other and continue the work that King began. He concedes that the path forward will not be easy, and they must pray for the nation and for the compassion needed to handle such a tragedy without violence or further hatred or divisiveness.
Themes and Rhetorical Strategies: appeal to ethos and pathos, unity, compassion/understanding

To provide **rhetorical support** is to support generalizations, claims, and arguments with examples, details, and other evidence. Because these rhetorical appeals are present in nearly all kinds of informative texts, students should receive significant instruction in, and practice at, identifying various appeals and their purpose in context. In rhetoric, writers can appeal to the audience in three main ways:

HELPFUL HINT

The goal of rhetorical instruction is to equip students with the skills to recognize, interpret, and evaluate rhetoric so that they can make informed decisions that are not clouded by the subtle influence of others.

- logical appeals (logos)
- emotional appeals (pathos)
- ethical appeals (ethos)

In Kennedy's speech quoted above, the young politician relies heavily on pathos—emotional appeal—to remind his audience that violence is unnecessary and that compassion and love can overcome it. As consumers of popular media, students need to understand that they do not have to be convinced by rhetoric: they can withhold their judgments and are free to disagree with some or all of what they read or hear. In fact, an audience can appreciate the craft, artistry, or power of a rhetorical text and still choose not to be persuaded.

PRACTICE QUESTION

Question 6 refers to the speech "Tribute to the Dog" by George Graham Vest.

The one absolutely unselfish friend that man can have in this selfish world, the one that never deserts him, the one that never proves ungrateful or treacherous is his dog. A man's dog stands by him in prosperity and in poverty, in health and in sickness. He will sleep on the cold ground, where the wintry winds blow and the snow drives fiercely, if only he may be near his master's side. He will kiss the hand that has no food to offer. He will lick the wounds and sores that come in encounters with the roughness of the world. He guards the sleep of his pauper master as if he were a prince. When all other friends desert, he remains. When riches take wings, and reputation falls to pieces, he is as constant in his love as the sun in its journey through the heavens.

6) What rhetorical device does George Graham Vest use?

   A. humor
   B. pathos
   C. allusion
   D. rhetorical question

AUDIENCE APPEAL

The principles that guide rhetorical practice rely heavily on a writer's understanding of the audience. To most effectively appeal to a particular audience, a writer must understand the audience's **perspective**—their point of view, frame of reference, position, or attitude toward an idea or occurrence. The writer has to appeal to them in ways that will be most appropriate for their unique perspectives.

HELPFUL HINT

An **argument from authority** or **appeal to authority** is a logical fallacy in which a person uses the opinion of an expert to support a claim without providing other evidence.

For example, a congressperson addressing a group of campaign supporters will appeal very differently to that audience as opposed to a congressional committee that the congressperson is trying to persuade. Good writers will select rhetorical strategies that appeal to their desired audience.

For example, the writer may include an **expert opinion** from an authority whom he knows a particular audience will respect. Writers may also use **testimonials**—

statements about the quality or value of a person, idea, or thing. When someone with a good reputation supports something, it strengthens an argument or claim. Students should learn to identify expert opinions and testimonials and the reasons writers might employ them in trying to convince an audience of a particular idea.

The language used by the writer should also be crafted to appeal to the technical knowledge of the audience. **Technical language** is related to a specific field of study and has a wide range, from computer technology to mechanics, engineering, and beyond. **Nontechnical language**, however, does not require specialized knowledge. Students should learn to identify technical and nontechnical language in an informative text; these can provide insight into the author's intended purpose and audience.

For example, a scientist writing for a group of peers might rely heavily on technical language since doing so will enhance the scientist's credibility as a professional in the field. On the other hand, if the scientist is writing to a popular audience, technical language might be a hindrance to the reader's understanding and will therefore be left out.

In all cases, students should be aware that writers of informative texts have a heightened awareness of their audience. This awareness allows them to shape their writing to be most effective for their intended purposes. By considering an author's specific choices, students can likely identify the author's audience and, subsequently, the author's purpose in writing.

PRACTICE QUESTION

To: All Employees

From: Dennis Frazier, Manager

Date: 08/28/17

Re: Email Communication

This is a reminder of our Email Policy.

Please refrain from sending company-related emails through personal email accounts. Use company-assigned email accounts for all correspondence.

Please email managers and team leaders about time off at least three days in advance. Last-minute emails or phone calls are not acceptable.

Please respond to emails within forty-eight hours, as some are time sensitive.

Thank you in advance for helping us all work better together!

7) Who is the intended audience of the memo?
    A. customers
    B. managers
    C. employees
    D. clients

STRATEGIES FOR DEVELOPING READING COMPREHENSION

Before beginning each new text, teachers should model and practice pre-reading strategies throughout reading instruction. One such strategy is **previewing** a text, which involves identifying the author, the genre, and the general subject matter before reading. It also includes reading headings and chapter titles, examining related graphics, researching the author and the context of the work (as is age appropriate), and anticipating the author's purpose.

Previewing general information about a text allows an active reader to use another pre-reading strategy: **setting a purpose**. A teacher might introduce each new text with a guiding question (For example: "What does it mean to be evil?") or a hypothetical situation that pushes students to examine their own value systems (For example: "Imagine you are a business owner. Should you be required to hire a certain number of individuals with disabilities?"). After facilitating a discussion about the question or scenario, the teacher directs students to a particular text to examine how the author or characters would respond. By setting a purpose for students' reading, the teacher guides them toward the thematic elements of the text. Students are encouraged to draw connections between the author's choices and the overall message.

Before reading a new text, and throughout the reading process, students should also make predictions about what they are reading. A **prediction** is a kind of inference that is concerned with what is going to happen next. Making predictions is a valuable active reading skill because it requires readers to be constantly aware of what is going on in the text as well as what authors may be foreshadowing through their specific choices.

In addition to making predictions as they read, students should be thinking about their own level of understanding, also known as metacognition. In **metacognition**, readers reflect on what they are thinking as they read. This helps to immediately identify any confusion or uncertainty. Readers who are aware of their thought processes are able to recognize and react when there is a breakdown in understanding. Part of metacognition in reading is using **fix-up or fix-it-up strategies**. Active readers apply these strategies when they realize they do not understand what they are reading. Common fix-up strategies include

- slowing down the reading pace;
- rereading the section in question;
- reading beyond the text in question to see if confusion is cleared up;
- using text clues;
- illustrations/graphic elements;
- text features (bold words, italics, headings, relevant punctuation);

- figuring out the meaning of unfamiliar words;
  - using context clues/words around the confusing word;
  - using picture clues;
  - using a resource to look up the word or words;
- asking a peer or teacher for assistance.

Annotating is another important strategy that takes place during reading. To provide effective instruction in annotation and ensure that students are mastering the skill, teachers should set clear guidelines and expectations. For example, a teacher might ask students to make **VISA annotations**. This involves having the students note

- interesting or new **v**ocabulary;
- important **i**nferences;
- helpful **s**ummaries;
- and brief **a**nalyses.

Other annotating strategies include

- underlining or highlighting main ideas or important information;
- circling key words;
- placing question marks next to confusing parts that might need further attention;
- writing notes in the margins.

Questioning is another way students can develop overall comprehension of a text. The reader asks and then answers questions about what has been read. Questioning occurs on three levels:

1. **Literal questions** are based on explicit information in the text and require only recall or identification of information from the text.

> On what day did Mark send the letter?

2. **Inferential questions** are based on implicit information in the text. These questions require students to make an inference, prediction, or draw a conclusion.

> What will Mark most likely do after he sends the letter?

3. **Evaluative questions** require readers to form an opinion on the text. Students will need to understand explicit information and then consider how they feel about this information.

> What do I think about Mark's action in sending the letter?

Summarization is a strategy to help readers determine what is important in the text. Using their own words, readers reduce a text or section of text to its main points or central ideas. This is done by skipping insignificant details and redundancies and looking for general ideas rather than specific facts and examples. Student-produced summaries can provide valuable insight into comprehension levels:

▶ Students who actively comprehend what they read will produce accurate summaries.

▶ Those who struggle with comprehension may leave out important ideas or leave in unnecessary information.

Summaries should be used throughout the study of a text and in the post-reading process to gauge how well students understood the basic ideas of the work. Teachers can encourage students to engage with the text using other post-reading strategies, such as having them **reflect** on their experiences with the text and write formal or informal responses. They may also ask students to return to the guiding question, which synthesizes their understanding of the text and its thematic and cultural relevance.

Students can also **make connections** between the text, themselves (text-to-self), the world (text-to-world), and other literature (text-to-text). The use of **text evidence** should be encouraged in any post-reading exercise, even in students' personal responses. It is important that their conclusions and understandings are fully informed and truly based in the text itself. Examination of textual evidence is an essential part of the process of constructing meaning.

> **DID YOU KNOW?**
>
> As readers consider textual evidence, they may change or expand their original interpretations.

PRACTICE QUESTION

8) What is an example of a metacognitive practice?

   A. a reader asking himself questions while reading
   B. a reader taking notes during a lecture about the historical background of a text that will soon be read
   C. a teacher providing pop quizzes to determine who has read a text
   D. a teacher explaining the characteristics of a given genre before students are asked to comprehend the genre

NONFICTION INSTRUCTIONAL STRATEGIES

Comprehension strategies for nonfiction texts are similar to those for fiction texts, though nonfiction texts might be less predictable in purpose and structure. Expository texts aim to teach something to the reader, which means that students are learning something new from a factual perspective while also analyzing rhetorical techniques. Many of the strategies previously mentioned for literary texts can also be used for nonfiction texts, but there are additional considerations.

Students will encounter nonfiction texts more often than fiction texts both across the curriculum and in their everyday lives. They should therefore be given plenty of strategies for overall comprehension of nonfiction texts. By helping students draw connections between the text and what they already know, it is constructive for teachers to help students tap into or activate background knowledge. Some effective methods to accomplish this include the following:

- A **brainstorm** web is used by writing the subject of the text in the center and encouraging students to fill in the rest of the web with information they already know about the topic.

- An **ABC brainstorm** can be done in small groups or as a class. Students write one word or phrase they already know about the topic for each letter of the alphabet.

- In **free brainstorm** students are asked to freely write down (or draw) what they already know about a topic.

Students should be taught to use various **annotation** strategies and encouraged to mark up the text, write in the margins, or use sticky notes. **Text coding** can help students develop metacognition skills:

- I = I already know this
- X = not what I expected
- * = important
- ? = question about this
- ?? = really confused by this
- ! = surprising
- L = learned something new
- RR = section needs to be reread

> **HELPFUL HINT**
>
> Collaborative learning strategies are effective in tackling challenging nonfiction texts. Students can be divided into pairs for reading activities or placed in larger groups where each member works on a different part of the text.

In addition to annotating, students can be prompted to use systematic **note-taking strategies:**

- completing a full or partial outline of the text from a template

- using two-column notes where students put main ideas on one side and important details on the other (known as the **split-page method**, or **two-column method**)
- using the **Cornell method** of note-taking whereby each page is divided into keywords, notes, and summary (see Figure 2.3)

Finally, students will benefit from a toolbox of fix-up strategies to use when comprehension breaks down. These might be similar to strategies used for fiction texts:

- Students should know when and how to use the glossary in each textbook.
- Students should have access to a dictionary appropriate for their age and skill level to consult as needed.
- Students should know whom to go to and how to ask for assistance when they have exhausted all their independent strategies.

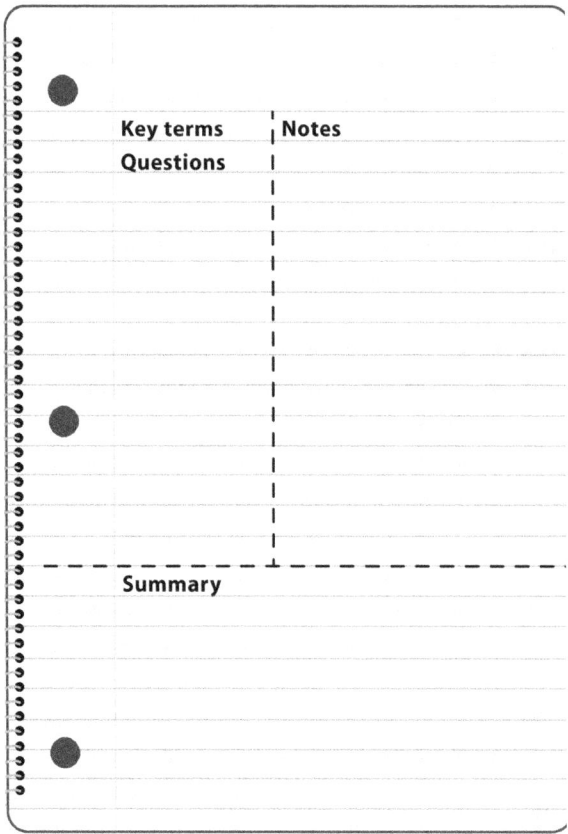

Figure 2.3. Cornell Method for Taking Notes

PRACTICE QUESTION

9) An eighth-grade teacher wants to activate students' background knowledge before reading a nonfiction passage on space exploration.

Which of the following activities BEST meets this goal?

A. asking students to freewrite a story set in outer space with extraterrestrial characters

B. having students construct a Milky Way galaxy out of construction paper and glitter

C. having students think about careers of the future that may be possible because of space exploration

D. asking students to write down three things they know about space exploration

SELECTING TEXTS

Finding a balance between the complexity of a text and a student's level of literacy development can be challenging. Many programs recognize this challenge and structure goal-setting and student assessments in a growth-over-time approach. Regardless of the milestones laid out by a school or district, teachers should encourage students to tackle ever-more sophisticated texts as they develop the foundational skills they need to take on new challenges. This, however, does not mean pushing students beyond what they can decode.

Giving students developmentally inappropriate texts may lead to a lack of confidence and less interest in, and enthusiasm for, reading. It can also lead to bad habits, such as guessing at or skipping unfamiliar words instead of trying to decode or asking for help. Many factors contribute to a text's complexity. In determining appropriateness, educators should evaluate texts based on both qualitative and quantitative measures and their match to the reader.

> **HELPFUL HINT**
>
> MetaMetrics also offers Lexile measures for Spanish-language texts.

Quantitative measurements include anything for which a number can be calculated, such as word frequency, the lengths of words and sentences, average syllables per word, and so on. Quantitative measurements can help calculate a range or score that is assigned to a text. For example, **MetaMetrics** is a company that uses word frequency and sentence length in an equation to yield a score. Scores are assigned to both readers and texts. Those assigned to readers typically come from standardized tests and measure current level of reading ability; these are called **reader measures.**

> **HELPFUL HINT**
>
> Lexile measures are only effective for texts that follow a typical structure. They are not effective for poetry and drama—these types of texts must be measured for complexity using other methods.

MetaMetrics also assigns **Lexile ranges** to texts called "Lexile text measures" or "Lexile measures." While these ranges do not have a direct correlation to grade level, educators can use charts created by MetaMetrics and/or a state or district to find the typical Lexile ranges for a given grade.

Table 2.3. Lexile Reader and Text Measures for Grades 1 – 12

Grade	Reader Measures, Midyear 25th to 75th Percentile This is the typical range of reading ability for students in each grade. These measures are designed to help compare a student's level to a typical range; they are not intended to be standards.	Text Measures These text measures have been revised from previous measures to better align with the Common Core State Standards for English Language Arts to ensure that students will meet these standards and be "college and career ready" by the end of high school.
1	BR120L to 295L	190L to 530L
2	170L to 545L	420L to 650L
3	415L to 760L	520L to 820L
4	635L to 950L	740L to 940L
5	770L to 1080L	830L to 1010L
6	855L to 1165L	925L to 1070L
7	925L to 1235L	970L to 1120L
8	985L to 1295L	1010L to 1185L
9	1040L to 1350L	1050L to 1260L
10	1085L to 1400L	1080L to 1335L
11 and 12	1130L to 1440L	1185L to 1385L

Other metrics for measuring the readability of a text include scales such as the **Flesch-Kincaid Grade Level,** the **Gunning Fog Index,** and the **SMOG Index.** A specific program or school may also use another proprietary tool, such as the Accelerated Reader Bookfinder or Scholastic's Guided Reading Leveling Resource Chart.

Beyond the quantitative measures determined by Lexile and others are **qualitative measures,** such as

- ▸ the layout of the text (illustrations, text size);
- ▸ the overall text structure (simple narrative chronology, more advanced argumentative essay);

- sentence structure (prevalence of simple or more complex sentences);
- levels of meaning (whether ideas are communicated explicitly or implicitly);
- knowledge demand (the cultural knowledge or other ideas that the reader must already know).

No single measure of any text can determine appropriateness for all students. For example, Lexile ranges do not account for mature subject matter. Teachers also need to differentiate literacy instruction in the classroom. Whichever strategy a program uses to address individualization of reading instruction, teachers must find just the right level of text complexity where students are challenged but not frustrated. Text complexity is highly individualized and should be matched to the instructional task:

- Texts at the **independent reading level** (for independent reading) require students to read with 99 percent accuracy and 90 percent comprehension. These are generally texts just "below" a student's reading level.

- **Instructional reading level** texts are used for teacher-guided instruction and are typically read at 85 percent accuracy with over 75 percent comprehension. These texts are usually "at" the student's reading level.

- **Frustration level** texts are those read at less than 85 percent accuracy and less than 50 percent comprehension. These texts are generally "above" a student's reading level and are not recommended. New research, however, suggests that such texts might be effective in paired reading activities with proficient readers.

In addition to selecting texts based on text measures, educators should consider other factors that depend on age. The following questions should guide the selection of texts for students:

- Are texts aligned to instructional goals?
- Are texts at the appropriate level (instructional or independent) for the planned activity?
- Are texts relevant and aligned to student interests?
- Do texts promote deep comprehension or analysis?
- Do texts contain highly specialized or nuanced vocabulary that students may not be familiar with?
- Do texts offer **multimodal elements** (appealing to different modes of communication such as written text, spoken language, and visual images) that might be relevant for instructional objectives?

When students are **self-selecting texts** or choosing something to read based on their own interests, they may still need scaffolding from educators. Knowing a student's personality, interests, and independent reading level can be helpful in this regard; however, even independent reading levels can evolve. Some students may seek out and enjoy more challenging texts, while others become frustrated at that level. Knowledge of the individual student should guide suggestions.

PRACTICE QUESTION

10) One disadvantage of relying on Lexile level as the sole indicator of text appropriateness is that

    A. it is only applicable to students whose first language is English.
    B. it fails to account for qualitative text features.
    C. it does not encourage the reading of rigorous texts.
    D. it can only be used to measure fiction texts.

Answer Key

1) B — Supporting text evidence is key to confirming answers on such a test and in confirming the author's purpose.

2) A — Emerson begins by making a general assertion about language and then goes on to provide specific examples of words that support his assertion.

3) B — The author states, "Ignored by the government, an activist group known as 'Indians of All Tribes' sailed to Alcatraz in the early morning hours with eighty-nine men, women, and children." The author goes on to describe the nineteen-month occupation of the island.

4) B — Options A, C, and D are listed as advantages of using subcontracting services (introduced after the signal words for example). Uncertainly about the legal definition of employment is given later as one of the disadvantages of using subcontracting services.

5) C — This is a red herring—a totally unrelated issue is being brought up.

6) B — The author is using pathos to appeal to the audience's feelings of love and appreciation toward devoted dogs.

7) C — The memo addresses "All Employees" in the heading segment.

8) A — When readers ask themselves questions as they read, they are monitoring their own understanding.

9) D — Having students write down what they already know about the topic (in this case, space exploration) will help them retrieve background information to set them up for more successful comprehension of the passage.

10) B — Lexile measures only account for quantitative text features like word and sentence lengths; they do not measure content, knowledge demands, and so on.

Language

The importance of verbal communication skills cannot be overstated: email communication, professional reports, court documents, business memos, and all other forms of written correspondence require a certain level of language expertise in order to be most effective.

While the many rules and guidelines of English language usage may be challenging for writers, the study of these structures can increase confidence in verbal communication—a benefit that will extend to nearly all areas of life.

GRAMMAR

Grammar refers to the structures and systems that make up a language. The **parts of speech** play unique roles in the context of a sentence and are the building blocks of sentences, paragraphs, and entire texts. Though some words fall easily into one category or another, many can function as different parts of speech based on their usage within a sentence. There are eight parts of speech typically defined by grammarians:

- nouns
- pronouns
- verbs
- adverbs
- adjectives
- conjunctions
- prepositions
- interjections

Syntax is the study of how words are combined to create sentences. In English, words are used to build phrases and clauses, which are combined to create sentences. By varying the order and length of phrases and clauses, writers can create sentences that are diverse and interesting. **Mechanics** describes those rules that govern the minutia of written English: punctuation, capitalization, and spelling while **usage conventions** guide writers and speakers more broadly in the area of word choice to ensure accuracy and agreement within a sentence.

> **HELPFUL HINT**
>
> **Prescriptivism** encourages language usage that observes grammatical correctness and adheres strictly to time-honored rules. **Descriptivism** argues that language should be taught in a way that mirrors how it is used in a day-to-day social context.

Nouns and Pronouns

Nouns are people, places, or things; the subject of a sentence is typically a noun. For example, in the sentence "The hospital was very clean," the subject, *hospital*, is a noun because it is a place. Nouns can be divided into many categories:

- common nouns (chair, car, house)
- proper nouns (Julie, David)
- abstract nouns (love, intelligence, sadness)
- concrete nouns (paper clip, bread, person)
- compound nouns (brother-in-law, roller coaster, toothpaste)
- noncountable nouns (money, water)
- countable nouns (dollars, cubes)
- verbal nouns (writing, diving)

Pronouns stand in for nouns and can be used to make sentences sound less repetitive. For example, in the sentence, "Sam stayed home from school because Sam was not feeling well," the name *Sam* appears twice in the same sentence. Instead of repeating the name *Sam*, the author can use the pronoun *he*:

> Sam stayed home from school because he was not feeling well.

Based on their role in a sentence, pronouns can be divided into categories as described in Table 3.1.

Table 3.1. Categories of Pronouns

Category	Function	Example
Personal pronouns	act as subjects or objects in a sentence	She received a letter.
Possessive pronouns	indicate possession	The car is mine.

Category	Function	Example
Reflexive/intensive pronouns	intensify a noun or reflect back upon a noun	I made the dessert myself.

Table 3.2. Personal, Possessive, and Reflexive/Intensive Pronouns

Case	First Person		Second Person		Third Person	
	singular	plural	singular	plural	singular	plural
Subject	I	we	you	you (all)	he, she, it	they
Object	me	us	you	you (all)	him, her, it	them
Possessive	mine	ours	yours	yours	his, her, its	theirs
Reflexive/intensive	myself	ourselves	yourself	yourselves	himself, herself, itself	themselves

Relative pronouns begin dependent clauses. Like other pronouns, they may appear in subject or object case, depending on the clause:

Charlie, who made the clocks, works in the basement.

Table 3.3. Relative Pronouns

Pronoun Type	Subject	Object
person	who	whom
thing	which, that	which, that
possessive	whose	whose

Interrogative pronouns begin questions:

Who worked last evening?

Table 3.4. Interrogative Pronouns

Interrogative Pronoun	Example
who	Who lives there?
whom	To whom shall I send the letter?
what	What is your favorite color?
where	Where do you go to school?

continued on next page

Table 3.4. Interrogative Pronouns (continued)

Interrogative Pronoun	Example
when	When will we meet for dinner?
which	Which movie would you like to see?
why	Why are you going to be late?
how	How did the ancient Egyptians build the pyramids?

Demonstrative pronouns (this, that, these, those) point out or draw attention to something or someone. They can also indicate proximity or distance:

> This is my apartment
>
> Give those to me later.

Because pronouns take the place of nouns, they need to agree in number with the noun they replace.

> The teachers are going to have a pizza party for their students.

Traditionally, pronouns must also agree in gender with the noun they are replacing; however this rule has become less stringent in recent years as ideas about gender identification continue to shift. The intentional use of *they* when referring to a singular noun is becoming more commonplace and accepted. Alternatively, sentences can be rewritten to avoid the use of gender-specific pronouns.

> **Traditional:** If a student forgets his or her homework, he or she will not receive a grade.
>
> **Use of singular** *they*: If a student forgets their homework, they will not receive a grade.
>
> **Rewritten with a plural antecedent:** Students who forget their homework will not receive a grade.

Pronouns should also be used carefully to avoid ambiguity in sentences. In the example below, it's unclear who *she* refers to. The sentence needs to be rewritten for clarity:

> **Incorrect:** After the teacher spoke to the student, she realized her mistake.
>
> **Correct:** After Mr. White spoke to the student, she realized her mistake.
>
> (*She* and *her* refer to the student.)
>
> **Correct:** After speaking to the student, the teacher realized her own mistake.
>
> (*Her* refers to the teacher.)

PRACTICE QUESTIONS

I have lived in Minnesota since August, but I still don't own a warm coat or gloves.

1) Which of the following lists includes all of the nouns in the above sentence?
   A. coat, gloves
   B. I, coat, gloves
   C. Minnesota, August, coat, gloves
   D. I, Minnesota, August, warm, coat, gloves

2) In which of the following sentences do the nouns and pronouns NOT agree?
   A. After we walked inside, we took off our hats and shoes and hung them in the closet.
   B. The members of the band should leave her instruments in the rehearsal room.
   C. The janitor on duty should rinse out his or her mop before leaving for the day.
   D. When you see people in trouble, you should always try to help them.

VERBS

Verbs express action (*run, jump, play*) or state of being (*is, seems*). Verbs can stand alone, or they can be accompanied by **helping verbs**, which are used to indicate tense. **Verb tense** indicates the time of the action. The action may have happened in the past, may be occurring in the present, or might take place in the future. The action may have been **simple** (occurring once) or **continuous** (ongoing). The **perfect** and **perfect continuous** tenses describe when actions occur in relation to other actions.

HELPFUL HINT

Helping verbs include: *is, am, are, was, were; be, being, been; has, had, have; do, does, did; should, would, could; will.*

Table 3.5. Verb Tenses

Tense	Past	Present	Future
Simple	I answered the question.	I answer your questions in class.	I will answer your question.
Continuous	I was answering your question when you interrupted me.	I am answering your question; please listen.	I will be answering your question after the lecture.
Perfect	I had answered all questions before class ended.	I have answered the questions already.	I will have answered every question before the class is over.
Perfect continuous	I had been answering questions when the students started leaving.	I have been answering questions for thirty minutes and am getting tired.	I will have been answering students' questions for twenty years by the time I retire.

Changing the spelling of a verb and/or adding helping verbs is called **conjugation**. In addition to tense, verbs are conjugated to indicate person. **Person** describes the relationship of the speaker to the subject of the sentence:

- first (*I, we*)
- second (*you*)
- third (*he, she, it, they*)

Number refers to whether the subject of the sentence is singular or plural. Verbs are conjugated to match the person and number of the subject; the conjugation of the verb must agree with the subject of the sentence. A verb that has not been conjugated is called an **infinitive** and begins with *to* (*to swim, to be*).

Table 3.6. Verb Conjugation (Present Tense)

Person	Singular	Plural
First person	I answer	we answer
Second person	you answer	you (all) answer
Third person	he/she/it answers	they answer

Sometimes, the subject and verb are separated by clauses or phrases. In the example below, the subject *cars* is separated from the verb by the relatively long phrase "that had been recalled by the manufacturer," making it more difficult to determine how to correctly conjugate the verb:

Incorrect: The cars that had been recalled by the manufacturer was returned within a few months.

Correct: The cars that had been recalled by the manufacturer were returned within a few months.

Verbs can also be classified by whether they take a **direct object**—a noun that receives the action of the verb. **Transitive verbs** require a direct object. In the sentence below, the transitive verb *throw* has a direct object (the ball):

The pitcher will throw <u>the ball.</u>

Intransitive verbs do not require a direct object. Verbs like *run*, *jump*, and *go* make sense without any object:

He will run.

Many sets of similar verbs include one transitive and one intransitive verb, which can cause confusion. Some troublesome verb combinations include *lie/lay*, *rise/raise*, and *sit/set*. The exam may test on these. Some commonly confused intransitive and transitive verbs are listed in Table 3.7.

Table 3.7. Intransitive and Transitive Verbs

Intransitive Verbs	Transitive Verbs
lie: to recline	lay: to put (lay something)
rise: to go or get up	raise: to lift (raise something)
sit: to be seated	set: to put (set something)
Intransitive Verbs	**Transitive Verbs**
Hint: These intransitive verbs have *i* as the second letter. "Intransitive" begins with *i*.	Hint: The word transitive begins with a *t*, and it TAKES an object.

PRACTICE QUESTIONS

3) Which of the following sentences contains an incorrectly conjugated verb?

   A. The brother and sister runs very fast.
   B. Neither Anne nor Suzy likes the soup.
   C. The mother and father love their new baby.
   D. Either Jack or Jill will pick up the pizza.

4) Which of the following sentences contains an incorrect verb tense?

   A. After the show ended, we drove to the restaurant for dinner.
   B. Anne went to the mall before she headed home.
   C. Johnny went to the movies after he cleans the kitchen.
   D. Before the alarm sounded, smoke filled the cafeteria.

> **HELPFUL HINT**
>
> Adverbs typically answer the questions *Where? When? Why? How? How often? To what extent? Under what conditions?*

ADJECTIVES AND ADVERBS

Adjectives modify, or describe nouns and pronouns. In English, adjectives are usually placed before the word they modify, although they can also come after a linking verb such as *is* or *smells*:

> The beautiful blue jade necklace will go perfectly with my dress.
>
> I think that lasagna smells delicious.

The suffixes *–er* and *–est* are used to modify adjectives in a comparison. The suffix *–er* is used when comparing two things, and the suffix *–est* is used when comparing more than two items:

Anne is <u>taller</u> than Steve, but Steve is <u>more coordinated.</u>

Of the five brothers, Jordan is the <u>funniest,</u> and Alex is the <u>most intelligent.</u>

Adjectives longer than two syllables are compared using *more* (for two things) or *most* (for three or more things):

Incorrect: Of my <u>two</u> friends, Clara is the <u>smartest.</u>

Correct: Of my <u>two</u> friends, Clara is <u>smarter.</u>

More and most should not be used with *-er* and *-est* endings. For example:

Incorrect: My <u>most warmest</u> sweater is made of wool.

Correct: My <u>warmest</u> sweater is made of wool.

Adverbs, which are often formed by adding the suffix *-ly*, modify any word (or set of words) that is not a noun or pronoun:

He quickly ran to the house next door.

(*Quickly* modifies the verb *ran*.)

PRACTICE QUESTIONS

The new chef carefully stirred the boiling soup and then lowered the heat.

5) **Which of the following lists includes all of the adjectives used in the above sentence?**

   A. new, boiling
   B. new, carefully, boiling
   C. new, carefully, boiling, heat
   D. new, carefully, boiling, lowered, heat

6) **Which of the following sentences contains an adjective error?**

   A. The new red car was faster than the old blue car.
   B. Reggie's apartment is in the tallest building on the block.
   C. The slice of cake was tastier than the brownie.
   D. Of the four speeches, Jerry's was the most long.

OTHER PARTS OF SPEECH

Prepositions set up relationships in time ("<u>after</u> the party") or space ("<u>under</u> the cushions") in a sentence. A preposition will always function as part of a **prepositional phrase**, which includes the preposition and the object of the preposition:

I ran over the river and through the woods.

Table 3.8. Common Prepositions

Prepositions	Compound Prepositions
along, among, around, at, before, behind, below, beneath, beside, besides, between, beyond, by, despite, down, during, except, for, from, in, into, near, of, off, on, onto, out, outside, over, past, since, through, till, to, toward, under, underneath, until, up, upon, with, within, without	according to, as of, as well as, aside from, because of, by means of, in addition to, in front of, in place of, in respect to, in spite of, instead of, on account of, out of, prior to, with regard to

Conjunctions join words into phrases, clauses, and sentences. There are three main types of conjunctions: coordinating, correlative, and subordinating. **Coordinating conjunctions** join together two independent clauses (complete thoughts). These can be remembered using the acronym *FANBOYS*: For, And, Nor, But, Or, Yet, So.

> **HELPFUL HINT**
>
> A preposition acts as an adverb when it provides more information about a verb: *Several days ago, we took the turkey bones outside because of the smelly garbage*. Here, the preposition explains where the bones were taken.

The following sentences use coordinating conjunctions:

> I will order lunch, but you need to go pick it up.
>
> Make sure to get sandwiches, chips, and sodas.

Correlative conjunctions *(whether/or, either/or, neither/nor, both/and, not only/but also)* work together to join items:

> Both the teacher and the students needed a break after the lecture.

Subordinating conjunctions join dependent clauses—thoughts that cannot stand alone as sentences—to the related independent clause. They usually describe a relationship between the two parts of the sentence, such as cause-effect or order and can appear at the beginning or in the middle of a sentence:

> We treat ourselves during football season to several orders because we love pizza.
>
> Because we love pizza, we treat ourselves during football season to several orders.

Table 3.9. Subordinating Conjunctions

Time	after, as, as long as, as soon as, before, since, until, when, whenever, while
Manner	as, as if, as though
Cause	because

continued on next page

Table 3.9. Subordinating Conjunctions (continued)

Condition	although, as long as, even if, even though, if, provided that, though, unless, while
Purpose	in order that, so that, that
Comparison	as, than

Interjections, like *wow* and *hey,* express emotion and are most commonly used in conversation and casual writing. They have no grammatical attachment to the sentence other than to add expressions of emotion. They may be punctuated with commas or exclamation points and may appear anywhere in a sentence. For example:

<u>Ouch!</u> He stepped on my toe.

PRACTICE QUESTIONS

Choose the word that BEST completes the sentence.

7) Her love _____ blueberry muffins kept her coming back to the bakery every week.

   A. to
   B. with
   C. of
   D. about

8) Christine left her house early on Monday morning, _____ she was still late for work.

   A. but
   B. and
   C. for
   D. or

Syntax

In English, words are used to build phrases and clauses, which are then combined to create sentences. Phrases and clauses are made up of a subject, a predicate, or both:

- The **subject** is what the sentence is about. It is usually a noun that performs the main action of the sentence, and it may be accompanied by modifiers.

- The **predicate** describes what the subject is doing or being. It contains the verb(s) and any modifiers or objects that accompany it.

A **phrase** is a group of words that communicates a partial idea and lacks either a subject or a predicate. Phrases are categorized based on the main word in the phrase. A **prepositional phrase** (discussed above) begins with a preposition and ends with an object of the preposition:

> The dog is hiding under the porch.

A **verb phrase** is composed of the main verb and its helping verbs:
> The chef would have created another soufflé, but the staff protested.

A **noun phrase** consists of a noun and its modifiers:
> The big, red barn rests beside the vacant chicken house.

Clauses contain both a subject and a predicate and can be either independent or **dependent**. An **independent** (or main) **clause** can stand alone as its own sentence:

> The dog ate her homework.

Dependent (or subordinate) **clauses** cannot stand alone as their own sentences. They start with a subordinating conjunction, relative pronoun, or relative adjective, which will make them sound incomplete:

> because the dog ate her homework

Table 3.10. Words That Begin Dependent Clauses

Subordinating Conjunctions	Pronouns and Adjectives
after, although, as, because, before, even if, even though, if, in order that, once, provided, since, so, so that, than, that, though, unless, until, when, whenever, where, whereas, wherever, whether, while	how, that, when, where, which, who, whoever, whom, whomever, whose, why

Table 3.11. Types of Clauses

Sentence type	Number of independent clauses	Number of dependent clauses	Example
Simple	1	0	San Francisco in the springtime is one of my favorite places to visit.

continued on next page

Table 3.11. Types of Clauses (continued)

Sentence type	Number of independent clauses	Number of dependent clauses	Example
Compound	2 or more	0	The game was canceled, but we will still practice on Saturday.
Complex	1	1 or more	I love listening to the radio in the car because I can sing along.
Compound-complex	2 or more	1 or more	I wanted to get a dog, but I have a fish because my roommate is allergic to pet dander.

Sentence errors fall into three categories:

> DID YOU KNOW?
>
> A sentence can be classified as simple, compound, complex, or compound-complex based on the type and number of clauses it has.

- fragments
- comma splices (comma fault)
- fused sentences (run-on)

A **fragment** occurs when a group of words lacks both a subject and verb as needed to construct a complete sentence or thought:

> **Incorrect:** Why am I not going to the mall? Because I do not like shopping.
> **Correct:** Because I do not like shopping, I will not plan to go to the mall.

A **comma splice** (comma fault) occurs when two independent clauses are joined with only a comma to "splice" them together. To fix a comma splice, a coordinating conjunction can be added, or a comma can be replaced with a semicolon:

> **Incorrect:** My family eats turkey at Thanksgiving, we eat ham at Christmas.
> **Correct:** My family eats turkey at Thanksgiving, and we eat ham at Christmas.
> **Correct:** My family eats turkey at Thanksgiving; we eat ham at Christmas.

Fused (run-on) sentences occur when two independent clauses are joined with no punctuation. Like comma splices, they can be fixed with a comma and conjunction or with a semicolon. For example:

> **Incorrect:** My sister lives nearby she never comes to visit.
> **Correct:** My sister lives nearby, but she never comes to visit.
> **Correct:** My sister lives nearby; she never comes to visit.

PRACTICE QUESTIONS

9) Which of the following options is a simple sentence?

    A. Elsa drove, while Erica navigated.
    B. Betty ordered a fruit salad, and Sue ordered eggs.
    C. Because she was late, Jenny ran down the hall.
    D. John ate breakfast with his mother, brother, and father.

10) Which of the following would NOT be an acceptable way to revise and combine the underlined portion of the following sentences?

    They receive an <u>annual pension payment. The amount of the pension</u> has been reviewed and changed a number of times.

    A. annual pension payment, the amount of which
    B. annual pension payment; the amount of the pension
    C. annual pension payment, the amount of the pension
    D. annual pension payment; the amount of each payment

HELPFUL HINT

Exclamation points have impact only in contrast to their frequency of usage: If the exclamation point is used frequently, each exclamation will be less impactful. If it is used sparingly, it will effectively draw the reader's attention.

PUNCTUATION

The main **punctuation marks** are periods, question marks, exclamation marks, colons, semicolons, commas, quotation marks, and apostrophes. There are three terminal punctuation marks used to end sentences. The **period** ends declarative (statement) and imperative (command) sentences:

> Sarah and I are attending a concert.

The **question mark** ends interrogative sentences:

> How many people are attending the concert?

Exclamation marks indicate that the writer or speaker is exhibiting intense emotion or energy:

> What a great show that was!

The **colon** and the **semicolon**, though often confused, have a unique set of rules about their respective uses. Both punctuation marks are used to join clauses, but the construction of the clauses and the relationship between them is different. The **semicolon** is used to show a general relationship between two independent clauses (IC; IC):

The disgruntled customer tapped angrily on the counter; she had to wait nearly ten minutes to speak to the manager.

Coordinating conjunctions (*FANBOYS*, discussed above) cannot be used with semicolons; however, conjunctive adverbs can be used following a semicolon:

She may not have to take the course this year; <u>however,</u> she will eventually have to sign up for that specific course.

The **colon,** somewhat less limited than the semicolon in its usage, is used to introduce a list, a definition, or a clarification. The clause preceding the colon must be an independent clause, but the clause that follows does not have to be:

Incorrect: The buffet offers three choices that include: ham, turkey, or roast.
Correct: The buffet offers three choices: ham, turkey, or roast.
Correct: The buffet offers three choices that include the following: ham, turkey, or roast.

Note that neither the semicolon nor the colon should be used to set off an introductory phrase from the rest of the sentence:

Incorrect: After the trip to the raceway; we realized that we should have brought earplugs.
Incorrect: After the trip to the raceway: we realized that we should have brought earplugs.
Correct: After the trip to the raceway, we realized that we should have brought earplugs.

The **comma** is a complicated type of punctuation that can serve many different purposes in a sentence. Comma placement is often an issue of style, not mechanics, meaning there may be more than one correct way to write the sentence. There are, however, a few important hard-and-fast comma rules, which are outlined in Table 3.12.

Table 3.12. Rules for Comma Usage

Rule	Example Sentence(s)
Commas should be used to separate two independent clauses along with a coordinating conjunction (FANBOYS).	Khalid ordered the steak, <u>but</u> Bruce preferred the ham.
Commas should be used to separate coordinate adjectives (two different adjectives that describe the same noun).	The <u>shiny, regal</u> horse ran majestically through the wide, open field.
Commas should be used to separate items in a series.	The list of groceries included <u>cream, coffee, doughnuts, and tea.</u>

Rule	Example Sentence(s)
Commas should be used to separate introductory words, phrases, and clauses from the rest of the sentence.	• <u>Slowly,</u> Nathan became aware of his surroundings after the concussion. • <u>Within an hour,</u> the authorities will descend on the home. • <u>After Alice swam the channel,</u> nothing intimidated her.
Commas should be used to set off appositive phrases—descriptors that are not needed for the sentence to make sense grammatically.	• Estelle, <u>our newly elected chairperson</u>, will be in attendance. • Ida, <u>my neighbor,</u> watched the children for me last week.
Commas should be used to set off titles of famous individuals.	Charles, <u>Prince of Wales,</u> visited Canada several times in the last ten years.
Commas should be used to set off the day and month of a date.	I was born on <u>February 16, 1958,</u> in Minnesota.
Commas should be used in numbers of more than four digits.	We expect <u>25,000</u> visitors to the new museum.

Quotation marks are used for many purposes. They enclose direct quotations in a sentence. Terminal punctuation that is part of the quotation goes inside the marks; terminal punctuation that is part of the larger sentence goes outside:

> She asked him menacingly, "Where is my peanut butter?"
> What is the original meaning of the phrase "king of the hill"?

In American English, commas are used to set quotations apart from the surrounding text and are placed inside the marks:

> "Although I find him tolerable," Arianna wrote, "I would never want him as a roommate."

While titles of longer works, like novels and anthologies, are italicized, quotation marks enclose titles of short, or relatively short, literary works such as short stories, chapters, and poems:

> For English class, we read "The Raven" by Edgar Allan Poe.

Quotation marks set off words used in a special sense or for a nonliterary purposes:

> The shady dealings of his Ponzi scheme earned him the ironic name "Honest Abe."

Apostrophes (sometimes referred to as single quotation marks) have a number of different uses: they show possession; they replace missing letters, numerals, and signs; they form plurals of letters, numerals, and signs in certain instances. Like commas, there are a number of rules for the correct usage of apostrophes, some of which are described in Table 3.13.

> **IMPORTANT WORKS**
>
> "The Raven"
> **Author:** Edgar Allan Poe
> **Publication Date:** 1845
> **Summary:** A man passes the time by reading in his room while grieving his dead love interest, Lenore. He hears a knock at the door and calls out to her, but no one is there. A knock on the window follows, so the man opens it, and a raven flies in and perches atop a bust of the Greek goddess Athena. The man asks the raven his name, and the raven replies, "nevermore." The raven continues this utterance, and the man wonders if the bird is trained to say this word. Still thinking of Lenore, the man asks the bird if his grief will end and if he will see her again in heaven, but the raven says again, "nevermore." He angrily demands that the bird leave, but it refuses and stays upon the bust forever.
> **Themes, Motifs, and Symbols:** the raven as a symbol of loss/grief, supernatural, futility, death

Table 3.13. Rules for Apostrophe Usage

Rule	Examples
To signify possession by a singular noun not ending in s, add 's.	boy → boy's
To signify possession by a singular noun ending in s, add 's.	class → class's
To signify possession by an indefinite pronoun not ending in s, add 's.	someone → someone's
To signify possession by a plural noun not ending in s, add 's.	children → children's
To signify possession by a plural noun ending in s, add only the apostrophe.	boys → boys'
To signify possession by singular, compound words and phrases, add 's to the last word in the phrase.	everybody else → everybody else's
To signify joint possession, add 's only to the last noun.	John and Mary's house
To signify individual possession, add 's to each noun.	John's and Mary's houses
To signify missing letters in a contraction, place the apostrophe where the letters are missing.	do not → don't

Rule	Examples
To signify missing numerals, place the apostrophe where the numerals are missing.	1989 → '89
To demonstrate possession or form a contraction with a numeral, add 's; only use for pluralization when the absence of an apostrophe would create confusion.	• Music from the 1980s is my favorite. • Mind your p's and q's. • The class earned a total of four As and sixteen Bs on the exam.

PRACTICE QUESTIONS

11) Which of the following sentences contains an error in punctuation?

   A. I love apple pie! John exclaimed with a smile.
   B. Jennifer loves Adam's new haircut.
   C. Billy went to the store; he bought bread, milk, and cheese.
   D. Alexandra hates raisins, but she loves chocolate chips.

12) Which punctuation mark correctly completes the following sentence?

*Sam, why don't you come with us for dinner_*

   A. .
   B. ;
   C. ?
   D. :

> **HELPFUL HINT**
>
> The comma before the conjunction in a series of items is called the Oxford, or serial, comma. It is optional and will not appear on the exam.

CAPITALIZATION

The most important rules for capitalization are listed in Table 3.14.

Table 3.14. Rules for Capitalization

Rule	Example
The first word of a sentence is always capitalized.	We will be having dinner at a new restaurant tonight.
The first letter of a proper noun is always capitalized.	We're going to Chicago on Wednesday.
Titles are capitalized if they precede the name they modify.	Kamala Harris, the vice president, met with President Biden.
Months are capitalized but not the names of the seasons.	Snow fell in March even though winter was over.

continued on next page

Table 3.14. Rules for Capitalization (continued)

Rule	Example
The names of major holidays should be capitalized. The word day is only capitalized if it is part of the holiday's name.	We always go to a parade on Memorial Day, but Christmas day we stay home.
The names of specific places should always be capitalized; general location terms are not capitalized.	We're going to San Francisco next weekend so I can see the ocean.
Titles for relatives should be capitalized when they precede a name but not when they stand alone.	Fred, my uncle, will make fried chicken, and Aunt Betty is going to make spaghetti.

PRACTICE QUESTION

13) Which of the following sentences contains an error in capitalization?

   A. My two brothers are going to New Orleans for Mardi Gras.
   B. On Friday we voted to elect a new class president.
   C. Janet wants to go to Mexico this Spring.
   D. Peter complimented the chef on his cooking.

Vocabulary

In addition to grammar, vocabulary plays an important role in language development. Students—both native English speakers and English language learners (ELLs)—benefit from continuous word acquisition, especially when they are seeing, learning, and studying new words in context. Teachers must therefore be able to support students by instructing them in the use of word clues and reference materials to acquire new vocabulary.

Phonics Instruction

Explicit phonics instruction is part of the early childhood and elementary education curricula; however, secondary ELA teachers should understand the basic principles of phonics instruction and apply these principles as they continue to develop students' reading, writing, and vocabulary skills.

Phonics is an age-old strategy for helping students read by connecting written language to spoken language or by correlating certain sounds with certain letters or groups of letters. Essential to phonics instruction is the concept of **letter-sound correspondence**—the knowledge that specific sounds are associated with specific letters. **Phonemes** are distinct units of sound and the basic units of language. There are

> **HELPFUL HINT**
>
> Fluency refers to the rate, accuracy, and expression of a text when read. It is an important measure of a student's reading development because it affects comprehension and reading. enjoyment.

twenty-six letters in the alphabet, and most researchers agree that there are at least forty-four phonemes in English. (Some letters represent different phonemes, and some phonemes are made up of more than one letter.)

Phonics instruction draws on the strategy of **decoding**, or the ability to pronounce the sounds of written words orally and understand their meaning. Some of the most common strategies for phonic instruction include the following:

- **Synthetic phonics** is one of the most common and effective types of phonics instruction. Students are explicitly taught to break down words into their component phonemes and sound them out.

- **Analytic phonics,** or implicit phonics, does not sound out each phoneme in a word; instead, students begin to recognize word families by identifying the initial sound (onset) and rime (the letters which follow the onset).

- **Embedded phonics,** or phonics through context, is an approach to phonics instruction that relies on incidental learning; whole texts are the primary curricular resources. Explicit phonics instruction is only used when students have trouble reading a particular word.

- **Phonics through spelling** is a combined approach whereby reading and spelling are taught in tandem. Students are taught to spell words phonetically by sounding them out or breaking them into their individual phonemes.

According to research, the synthetic phonics approach is the most universal method of phonics instruction that can meet the needs of the most learners. Research also indicates that **systematic phonics instruction** occurring in a particularly designed sequence is the most effective. Phonics instruction is also highly effective when it includes **connected texts**, or words in sentences and paragraphs instead of only in isolation or lists.

> **HELPFUL HINT**
>
> **Sight words** require no decoding because they are instantly recognized and read automatically. Young students will work on memorizing sight words with basic sound structures that cannot be sounded out.

PRACTICE QUESTION

14) A kindergarten teacher is working with a student to read a short sentence: He ran to the woods. The student becomes stuck on *woods*. Which question should the teacher ask to stay aligned with synthetic phonics instruction?

   A. What do the pictures tell you this word might be?

continued on next page

B. What sound do the letters in the word make?
C. Where would someone run?
D. What other words do you know that rhyme with *wood*?

Word Analysis

The human brain uses three cueing systems to determine the meaning of words: semantic, syntactic, and graphophonic. Together, these systems form word-analysis strategies, or **word-attack strategies**—methods of decoding unfamiliar words.

Semantic cues offer prompts to a word's meaning and are drawn from background knowledge or context clues. Since words are immediately retrieved from memory and processed, semantic cues are the brain's most efficient cueing system. Semantic cues rely on students to activate knowledge and make reasonable predictions and inferences regarding a word's meaning.

> **HELPFUL HINT**
>
> **Homographs** are words that are *spelled* the same but have different meanings; **homonyms** are words that *sound* the same but have different meanings. Students should be taught to use context clues to identify the meanings of homographs and homonyms they encounter while reading.

Semantic cues based on the text itself are called context clues. **Context clues** can be other words in the text or graphics. Students should be explicitly taught to identify other words in a sentence, paragraph, or passage that provide possible clues to the meaning of an unknown word. Students of all ages can also look to illustrations or charts to understand new words. This is particularly helpful with subject-specific vocabulary, such as terminology associated with organelles within plant cells.

Syntactic cues are based on the structure of language and regarded as the brain's second-most efficient cueing system while reading. They include sentence structure and word order, structural clues within words, and structural analysis of the word. A word's meaning can sometimes be clued or determined by its placement in a sentence. For example, figuring out whether a word is used as an adjective, noun, or verb can help with determining its meaning. Structural analysis of the word can also be a useful strategy. Students can decode compound words, for example, by breaking the word into its two component parts.

Structural clues within words such as affixes (prefixes and suffixes) and roots (base words with no affixes) can also offer clues to a word's meaning. This is sometimes referred to as **morphemic analysis,** or the analysis of morphemes (the smallest units of meaning within words). (Affixes and roots are discussed in more detail in the next section.)

The **graphophonic cueing** system is based on applying sound (phoneme)-symbol (grapheme or letter) knowledge while reading. It is the most basic level of decoding and tends to be the least efficient since its focus is on individual units (letters and letter patterns, for example) instead of larger chunks of text, like words and ideas.

For graphophonic cueing to be most effective, readers must have some knowledge of the word they are sounding out to make meaning. For example, a ninth-grade student might be able to apply graphophonic cueing to successfully sound out the word *meticulous*; however, this word is not truly decoded unless the student can use other clues to determine the word's meaning. For this reason, many educators use **whole-language** instruction, which does not use any cueing system smaller than the word level. In a whole-language approach, students must use semantic and syntactic cues as the only methods for decoding new words.

PRACTICE QUESTIONS

15) Which activity would MOST likely help students develop the knowledge to use semantic cues effectively?
    A. reading books that provide information on a variety of places and cultures
    B. underlining confusing sentences and diagramming them
    C. reading a text aloud twice, once to oneself and once to a partner
    D. encouraging students to increase their reading rate to retain more information

Practice question 16 is based on the following passage:

The Bastille, Paris's famous historic prison, was originally built in 1370 as a fortification, called a *bastide* in Old French, to protect the city from English invasion during the Hundred Years' War. It rose 100 feet into the air, had eight towers, and was surrounded by a moat more than eighty feet wide. In the seventeenth century, the government converted the fortress into a prison for upper-class felons, political disruptors, and spies. Residents of the Bastille arrived by direct order of the king and usually were left there to languish without a trial.

16) Which of the following phrases from the passage could be used as a context clue to help students determine the meaning of the word fortification?
    A. "surrounded by a moat more than eighty feet wide"
    B. "arrived by direct order of the king"
    C. "converted the fortress into an prison"
    D. "to protect the city from English invasion"

ROOT WORDS AND AFFIXES

Roots are the building blocks of all words: every word is either a root itself or has a root. The root is what is left when you strip away the prefixes and suffixes from a word. For example, if you take away the prefix *un–* from the word *unclear*, you have the root *clear*.

Roots are not always recognizable because they often come from Latin or Greek words, such as *nat*, a Latin root meaning "born." The word *native*, which refers to a person born in a referenced place, comes from this root. So does the word *prenatal*, meaning "before birth." It is important to keep in mind, however, that roots can have several spellings and do not always match the original definitions of words.

Prefixes are elements added to the beginning of a word, and **suffixes** are elements added to the end of a word; together they are known as **affixes.** They carry assigned meanings and can be attached to a word to completely change its meaning or enhance the word's original meaning. For example, in the word *prefix:*

Fix means "to place something securely."
Pre- means "before."
Therefore, *prefix* means "to place something before or in front of."

An example of a suffix can be found in the word *feminism*:

Femin is a root that means "female."
The suffix *-ism* means "act," "practice," or "process."
Therefore, *feminism* is the process of establishing equal rights for women.

A list of common roots, prefixes, and suffixes can be found in the appendix.

PRACTICE QUESTIONS

Which option offers the best definition of the underlined word in the following sentences?

17) The bellicose dog will be sent to training school next week.
    A. misbehaved
    B. friendly
    C. scared
    D. aggressive

18) The new menu rejuvenated the restaurant and made it one of the most popular spots in town.
    A. established
    B. invigorated
    C. improved
    D. motivated

Vocabulary Development

Vocabulary can—and should—be broadened through a variety of strategies. Vocabulary knowledge makes reading more expedient and fluent since readers can simply decode a word semantically without having to resort to other cueing systems. Vocabulary development should focus on retention, not memorization—the goal is for students to be able to not just recognize words but also understand and use them appropriately. Vocabulary is developed through one of two ways:

- **Incidental vocabulary learning** occurs while reading, either independently or through teacher-guided oral reading activities.

- **Intentional vocabulary teaching** requires educators to more explicitly direct vocabulary acquisition.

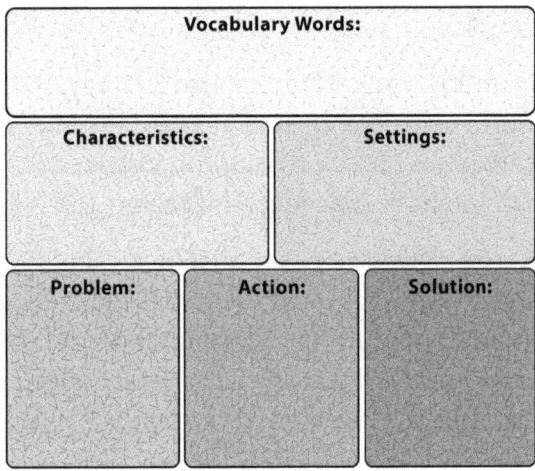

Figure 3.1. Predict-O-Gram

Strategies for intentional vocabulary teaching include the following:

Predict-O-Gram: Students are given a list of words and predict how they will be used in a text. This strategy can be used effectively for both fiction and nonfiction texts, though it is most often used with fiction since it can be easily integrated into existing knowledge about plot structure.

Semantic impressions: Students are given a list of words in the order they appear in the text. The definition of each word is then briefly discussed by the teacher. Students write their own stories using the words in the same order, using each word only once. Students then read the text and compare their finished stories to the original.

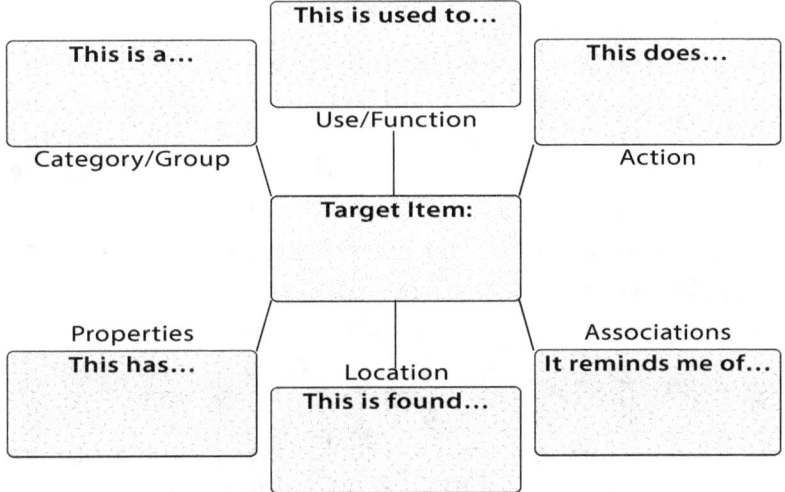

Figure 3.2. Semantic Feature Analysis

Semantic feature analysis: Also called a semantic grid, this strategy functions as a graphic organizer that helps students think deeply about the features or properties of each vocabulary word.

Frayer model: This is a specific type of semantic analysis with four grids on which students write the definition of a word, along with its characteristics, examples, and nonexamples.

List-group-label: In this semantic mapping strategy, students brainstorm all the words they can think of that relate to a particular topic. They then divide the list of words into subcategories based on common features. For example, words like *dorsal fin*, *gills*, and *teeth* might be placed in the category of "parts of a fish's body."

Possible sentences: Students are given a list of vocabulary words from the text they will read. They then write a "possible" sentence for each word, illustrating the word's possible meaning. After reading the text, students return to their possible sentences to see if they were accurate or if the sentences need to be changed based on the word's actual meaning as revealed in the text.

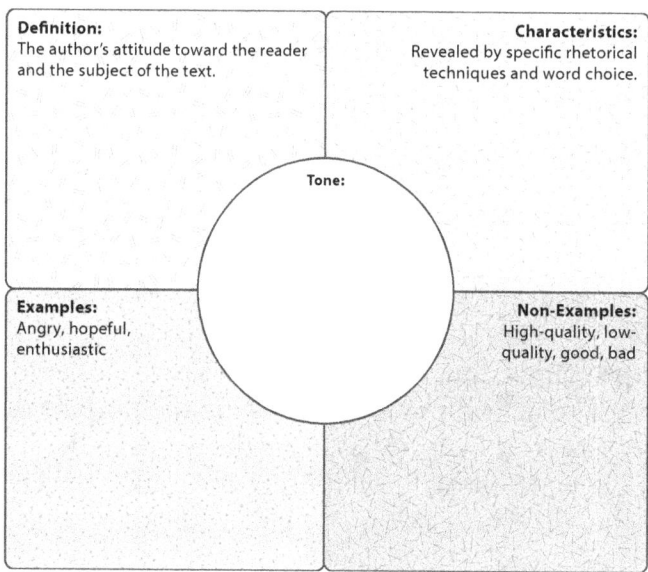

Figure 3.3. Frayer Model

OPIN: Short for *opinion*, this strategy is similar to a cloze exercise in which students fill in the blank with a word they think belongs in a sentence. Then, students break into groups to "defend" their word choice to other members of the group. This strategy helps reinforce other skills since students use context clues and background knowledge to justify their answers.

PRACTICE QUESTION

19) Which of the following exercises could best be used to incorporate vocabulary acquisition into a creative writing unit?

    A. list-group-label

B. OPIN
C. semantic impressions
D. semantic grids

Resources

Despite their best efforts, students will inevitably encounter a word that they cannot decipher based on usage alone. Thus, in order to assist students in the acquisition of new words, teachers must be knowledgeable about the tools and resources that are at their students' disposal in the modern age. Teachers must understand the purpose and usage of each kind of resource, the limits of the various tools, and the advantages and disadvantages of dependence on reference materials.

Spellcheckers come as a default on many word processing systems and can be helpful as a first line of defense against spelling (and even grammar) errors; however, spellcheckers should not be used in isolation since they are limited in their ability to catch certain kinds of errors. For example, a spellchecker might recognize *therre* as an incorrect spelling of *there,* but it would not recognize *their* as incorrect in context. Though improvements are always being made to automatic spelling and grammar checking technology, students would be prudent to continue doing their own editing as well.

Style manuals are guidebooks for general language usage and the documentation of sources within a written document, anthology, or field of study. While some style manuals exist to serve a general readership, like *The Chicago Manual of Style,* many serve specific audiences or professional groups, like the *Publication Manual of the American Psychological Association,* which is used in most social science publications. Students should be familiarized with some of the more common style manuals and be able to apply them to their own work.

Dictionaries provide the definitions of words along with a few other important details, such as a word's part of speech and other forms. Dictionaries are therefore especially useful tools for English language learners. With a good dictionary students can

- look up the meaning of a word;
- check the spelling of a word;
- check the plural of a noun or past tense of a verb;
- find out other grammatical information about a word;
- find the synonym or antonym of a word;
- check the part of speech of a word;
- find out how to pronounce a word;
- find out about the register of a word (formal or informal, for example);
- find examples of a word's usage.

Bilingual dictionaries can be used to translate words and/or phrases between two languages. While some bilingual dictionaries allow the user to translate only from one language to the other, many actually allow the reader to translate in both directions—to and from the secondary language.

A **thesaurus** is useful when considering alternate word choices. It provides synonyms and antonyms and helps writers vary their language or find just the right word to communicate a particular idea. Students should be taught, however, that a thesaurus should be used cautiously: replacing words for the sake of choosing ones that are interesting or more advanced can sometimes complicate the true meaning of a text. Enhancing word choice without overwriting is challenging but generally makes for the most effective writing. Indeed, as long as the voice of the writer is maintained, a thesaurus can become a tool to add creativity to the text. For example:

The man walked toward his house in the wind and snow.

Ineffective use of synonyms:

The fellow ambulated in the orientation of his household, against the strident gale and frigid precipitation.

Effective use of synonyms:

The man trudged toward his distant house, against the harsh wind and unrelenting snow.

A **glossary** is a list of terms and definitions found in a specific text and is usually located at the end of the book. Glossaries are common in textbooks and other technical publications.

Teachers should emphasize that these resources are designed to be tools for students, not substitutes for their own knowledge. For instance, after looking up a new word in the dictionary, students should make an effort to learn the word. Students may refer to these resources throughout their academic careers, but they should do their best to enhance their own knowledge.

PRACTICE QUESTION

20) A student in Mr. Moreno's class is writing an essay and needs to find a suitable replacement for the word justify. Where should the student look first?

    A. the dictionary
    B. a glossary
    C. a bilingual dictionary
    D. a thesaurus

SOCIOLINGUISTICS

In the United States alone, **language diversification** has led to interesting variances in usage across dialects, accents, regionalisms, and cultures: One area of the country may use the word *soda* while another area of the country may use the word *pop* or *coke*. One area may use the word *sneaker* while another may say *tennis shoe*. Certain areas of the country may say *grinder* to refer to a long sandwich while others may use the word *hero* or *sub*.

A writer should consider both **purpose** and **audience** in deciding whether to employ colloquialisms or adhere to prescriptive conventions. Proper prescriptive usage may be beneficial during a presentation to a potential investor, for example, but a campaign speech in a local town might be enhanced by the use of regionalisms.

Sociolinguistics is the study of language and its relation to society and culture. One reason sociolinguistics is important is because sociocultural factors determine **language policy,** which is what a government establishes to regulate which language(s) is/are spoken and where and when in a country. In countries with a multilingual population, the exclusion of or attempt to exclude languages can cause social and political conflict. Indeed, language has played a crucial part in the separatist movements of regions in many countries, namely Québec in Canada and the Basque in Spain.

Another important point of study in sociolinguistics is that of regional and social dialects. **Regional and social dialects** are varieties of a language that people in a certain region or social group speak. Dialects are real sociolinguistic phenomena studied and written about and easily heard by laypeople, but they also carry the weight of sociocultural stereotypes and prejudice. For example, in the United States, the "Southern drawl" is well-liked but often associated with ignorance in news, television, film, and literature.

When people of two or more language groups need to communicate, they often develop a **pidgin** language—a grammatically simplified mode of communicating that may use elements of both languages. A pidgin is not a person's native language; it is a language of necessity which allows speakers of different languages to communicate. The most common situation that would call for a pidgin would be trade, such as that which occurred with the development of Chinese Pidgin English when the British began to trade heavily in China in the eighteenth century.

> **HELPFUL HINT**
>
> If a pidgin language becomes nativized and people begin speaking it as a first language, it is then known as a **creole.** For example, the Gullah language spoken on the South Carolina coast is a creole.

Another area in which dialect plays a part is the idea of **World Englishes.** There are many varieties of English spoken in the world as first and other languages. In fact, after the United States, India has the world's highest number of English speakers.

Because of colonialization by England and the United States, many countries in the world speak English as a first or second language. Moreover, because of the prevalence of English as a *lingua franca* in global business, entertainment, commerce, and academia, many more people also learn to speak English as a second language. As the world becomes increasingly globally connected, both native English speakers and those speaking English as a second language must become accustomed to understanding these varying dialects of English.

Communicative competence means being able to speak a language appropriately in a social context as well as correctly in terms of rules and structure. Linguists break down communicative competence into four distinct areas:

- **Linguistic competence** refers to knowledge of the linguistic components of a language, such as syntax, semantics, and so on.

- **Sociolinguistic competence** means using the language in a socially appropriate way and includes understanding register—degrees of formality, differences in setting, appropriate context, and so on.

- **Discourse competence** deals with the knowledge of how to construct smaller units of language, like phrases and sentences, into cohesive works like letters, speeches, conversations, and articles.

- **Strategic competence** is the ability to recognize and repair instances of "communication breakdown" by strategic planning and/or redirecting.

PRACTICE QUESTION

21) Which of the four components of communicative competence would address the appropriate way for a student to speak to his school principal?

   A. linguistic competence
   B. sociolinguistic competence
   C. discourse competence
   D. strategic competence

ANSWER KEY

1) C — *Minnesota* and *August* are proper nouns, and *coat* and *gloves* are common nouns. *I* is a pronoun, and *warm* is an adjective that modifies coat.

2) B — "The members of the band" is plural, so the plural pronoun *their* should be used instead of the singular *her*.

3) A — Option A should read "The brother and sister run very fast." When the subject contains two or more nouns connected by *and*, the subject is plural and requires a plural verb.

4) C — Option C should read "Johnny will go to the movies after he cleans the kitchen." It does not make sense to say that Johnny does something in the past ("went to the movies") after doing something in the present ("after he cleans").

5) A — *New* modifies the noun *chef,* and *boiling* modifies the noun *soup. Carefully* is an adverb modifying the verb *stirred. Lowered* is a verb, and *heat* is a noun.

6) D — Option D should read "Of the four speeches, Jerry's was the *longest*." The word long has only one syllable, so it should be modified with the suffix –est, not the word *most*.

7) C — The correct preposition is *of.*

8) A — In this sentence, the conjunction joins together two contrasting ideas, so the correct answer is *but*.

9) D — Option D contains one independent clause with one subject and one verb. Options A and C are complex sentences because they each contain both a dependent and independent clause. Option B contains two independent clauses joined by a conjunction and is therefore a compound sentence.

10) C — This option creates a comma splice; the other options are all correct.

11) A — Option A should use quotation marks to set off a direct quote: "I love apple pie!" John exclaimed with a smile.

12) C — The sentence is a question, so it should end with a question mark.

13) C — *Spring* is the name of a season and should not be capitalized.

14) B — Asking about the sounds the letters make will help the student decode the word *woods* by sounding it out.

15) A — Reading a broad array of books builds background knowledge, which can then be applied and retrieved.

16) D — A fortification is a defensive structure meant to protect.

17) D — Both *misbehaved* and *aggressive* look like possible answers given the context of the sentence; however, the prefix *belli–*, which means "warlike," can be used to confirm that *aggressive* is the correct answer.

18)	B	All of the answer options could make sense in the context of the sentence, so it is necessary to use word structure to find the definition. The root *juven* means "young," and the prefix *re–* means "again," so *rejuvenate* means "to be made young again." The answer option with the most similar meaning is *invigorated,* which means "to give something energy."
19)	C	The semantic impressions strategy involves having students write a story with the words from the text.
20)	D	A thesaurus provides a list of synonyms and antonyms for each word.
21)	B	Sociolinguistic competence deals with using language in a socially appropriate way.

Writing and Research

At its most basic level—the sentence—the use of effective language is essential to effective communication. Beyond these basics, however, students must spend a significant amount of time both inside and outside of school developing the writing, speaking, and listening skills that will allow them to succeed in the adult world. An ELA classroom emphasizes building students' written communication skills, which extend far beyond the basics of grammar and vocabulary: producing meaningful writing is a task that requires extensive planning and revising.

THE RECURSIVE WRITING PROCESS

Students should understand that writing is a process—even professional writers put their work through several phases before releasing the finished product. A **recursive writing process** means that writers may return to a previously completed part of the process. Also known as the **authoring cycle,** this process includes several phases in which ideas are transformed into written form to effectively communicate meaning:

1. plan
2. draft
3. revise
4. edit
5. publish

The first step in planning is to **brainstorm** ideas, which can take many forms. Teachers might have the class generate ideas for topics and write them on the board or screen.

Students can then create their own **webs** or **outlines** to organize their ideas. This initial planning can help students formulate their overall point and supporting details.

Brainstorming activities can be based on a book the students have read, their opinion of the work ("I liked the book," "I did not like the book," "My favorite/least favorite part was …") and the reasons for their opinions. Students might also write a simple expository piece that introduces a topic and then uses supporting details to inform the reader. Brainstorming activities can also help students organize the events they want to describe when writing narratives.

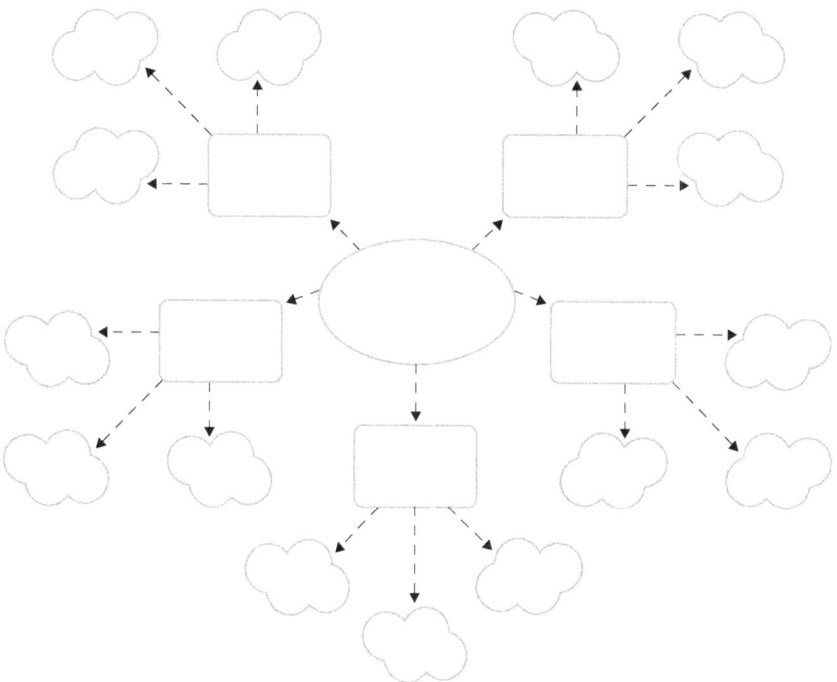

Figure 4.1. Brainstorming Web

After brainstorming, students **draft** their piece and connect their ideas with an introductory statement followed by the supporting and concluding sections. With scaffolding, students then go through a **revision** process where they address weaknesses in the writing, such as adding more supporting details or connecting words (because, also, then) to improve clarity. They can then **edit** for capitalization, punctuation, and spelling.

> **HELPFUL HINT**
>
> Teachers can support students in the revision process by giving them a simple checklist to help ensure they have met certain criteria. One such checklist is the **COPS mnemonic,** which stands for Capitalization, Organization, Punctuation, and Spelling.

Teachers can also use peer and teacher feedback as part of the revision process. Receiving feedback helps students understand that the main purpose of writing is to communicate ideas; having other readers offer their perceptions and suggestions is therefore an important part of revision.

Students should **publish** their work after the final copy is created, particularly if the writing project was significant in scope.

Having students read their work aloud is one simple and immediate way to publish a piece (as well as a way to link reading and writing), as is posting it on a classroom or school bulletin board. Teachers may have students organize and bind their work into a simple book using string or fasteners, or they may collect student work into a class-wide literary sampler.

I. The first paragraph introduces the reader to the topic (here, *Cats make better pets than dogs*).
   A. An anecdote may get a reader's attention; here, the writer could relate a personal story about an experience with a dog or cat.
   B. <u>Thesis statement</u>: While dogs are loyal and protective, cats are smarter, more affordable, independent, and cuter, so they make better pets.
II. Cats are smarter than dogs.
   A. Dogs often get sick from eating foreign objects, incurring costly vet bills; cats rarely eat such items.
   B. If dogs are left outside alone, they may get lost and are at risk of injury or death due to traffic; cats are able to protect themselves better and almost always find their way home.
III. Cats are easier to care for than dogs.
   A. Cats are smaller and lazier; they do not require walks.
   B. Cats can be left alone for several days with ample food, water, and litter; dogs require daily attention and thus a dog sitter.
IV. Cats are more pleasant to live with than dogs.
   A. Cats have softer fur and are therefore cuddlier.
   B. Cats are quieter than dogs; they meow, while dogs bark.
V. The final paragraph concludes the essay and discusses the broad implications of the issue.
   A. <u>Restatement of Thesis</u>: Even though dog ownership has many benefits, the convenience, affordability, and enjoyment cats offer make them the superior pet.
   B. With so much to offer, cats will surely become even more popular than they are today.

If a teacher uses student portfolios in the classroom, students can prepare their pieces for inclusion in a digital or physical folder. This may involve transcribing the piece digitally, adding illustrations, or matting it on construction paper.

Teachers should also emphasize that sharing work with others is an important part of publishing. This is also a great way to build a connection between home and school: students should be encouraged to share their work with parents or guardians. Teachers should also show student work samples or portfolios at parent conferences to further build the home–school connection.

PRACTICE QUESTION

1) A high school English teacher sponsors a creative writing club that meets weekly after school. He asks the reading specialist for advice on a high-impact way to publish student work and share it with the school community. What should the specialist suggest?

   A. invite administrators to attend one of the club meetings and listen to students read their work
   B. encourage students to read their pieces at home to their family members
   C. plan a digital or print literary journal that can be shared across the school
   D. teach students to use publishing and graphic design software to format their pieces

ORGANIZING WRITING

All students should know how to develop a thesis statement and organize their nonfiction writing to include an introduction, body, and conclusion. The thesis, or **thesis statement,** is central to the structure and meaning of an essay: it presents the writer's argument or position on an issue, concisely packaged into a one- or two-sentence statement. A strong, direct thesis statement is key to the organization of any essay and introduces its central idea and the main points that will be used to support that idea.

> **PROMPT:** Many high schools have begun to adopt 1:1 technology programs, meaning that each school provides every student with a computing device, such as a laptop or tablet. Educators who support these initiatives say that the technology allows for more dynamic collaboration and that students need to learn technology skills to compete in the job market. On the other hand, opponents cite increased distraction and the dangers of cyberbullying or unsupervised internet use as reasons not to provide students with such devices.
>
> *In your essay, take a position on this question. You may write about either one of the two points of view given, or you may present a different point of view on this question. Use specific reasons and examples to support your position.*
>
> Possible thesis statements
>
> 1) Providing technology to every student is good for education because it allows students to learn important skills such as typing, web design, and video editing, and it also gives students more opportunities to work cooperatively with their classmates and teachers.

> 2) I disagree with the idea that schools should provide technology to students because most students will simply be distracted by the free access to games and websites when they should be studying or doing homework.
>
> 3) By providing each student with a laptop or tablet, schools can help students apply technology to work more effectively with other students, communicate with teachers and classmates, and conduct research for class projects.

The purpose of an **introduction** is to set the stage for the essay. This is accomplished by capturing the reader's interest, introducing and providing context for the topic, and stating the central idea and main points of the essay. Usually the introductory paragraph ends with a thesis statement.

> Introduction Example
>
> Technology has changed massively in recent years, but today's generation barely notices—high school students are already experienced with the internet, computers, apps, cameras, cell phones, and more. It's inevitable that these technologies will begin to make their way into classrooms. Opponents of 1:1 technology programs might argue that students will be distracted or misuse the technology, but that is exactly why schools must teach them to use it. Students need to know how to navigate technology safely and effectively, and schools have a responsibility to ensure they learn these skills. By providing each student with a laptop or tablet, schools can help students learn how to apply technology to work more effectively with other students, communicate with teachers and classmates, and conduct research for class projects.

The **body** of the essay should consist of paragraphs that present the details that support the main idea. Each paragraph should be structurally consistent, beginning with a topic sentence to introduce the main idea, followed by supporting ideas and examples. No extra ideas unrelated to the paragraph's focus should appear. Transition words and phrases can be used to connect body paragraphs and improve the flow and readability of the essay.

> **HELPFUL HINT**
>
> The acronym *RENNS* can be used to recall the kinds of details that writers can use to support their main idea: Reasons, Examples, Names, Numbers, and Senses. By varying the types of details they use, writers can make text more interesting and convincing.

> Body Paragraph Example
>
> Technology can be a powerful tool for collaboration. When all of the students in a classroom have access to reliable laptops or tablets, they are able to share information and work together on projects more effectively. Students can communicate quickly via email, share files through a cloud service, and use a shared calendar for scheduling. They also have the opportunity to teach each other new skills since each student may bring to the group unique knowledge about particular apps or programs. When the availability of technology is limited or inconsistent, these opportunities are lost.

To end an essay smoothly, the author must compose a **conclusion** that reminds the reader of the importance of the topic and then restates the essay's thesis and supporting details. The writer should revisit the ideas in the introduction and thesis statement, but these ideas should not be simply repeated word-for-word. Rather, a well-written conclusion will reinforce the argument using wording that differs from the thesis statement but conveys the same idea. The conclusion should provide the essay with a sense of closure and leave the reader with a strong impression of its main idea.

<u>Conclusion Example</u>

As technology continues to change and become more incorporated into everyday life, students will need to adapt to it. Schools already teach young people a myriad of academic and life skills, so it makes sense that they would also teach students how to use technology appropriately. When technology is incorporated into schoolwork, students will learn to collaborate, communicate, and research more effectively. Providing students with their own devices is one part of this important task, and schools that do so should be supported.

PRACTICE QUESTION

2) What is the purpose of a thesis statement?
   A. to effectively conclude an essay
   B. to summarize the supporting details of an argument
   C. to present the writer's main argument
   D. to introduce the topic of an essay

WRITING WELL

In addition to learning how to craft an argument, students should learn how to effectively use language to present their ideas. Writing well means that the language and tone are appropriate for the purpose and audience of the writing task, the flow of ideas and the relationships among them are logical and clear, and the sentences are varied enough to keep the reader interested.

Transitions are words and phrases that help connect ideas throughout a text between sentences and paragraphs. They can be used to imply a range of relationships, including cause and effect, sequence, contradictions, and continuance of an idea. The consistent and creative use of transitions helps essays flow logically from one idea to the next and will make them easier for the reader to follow.

Table 4.1. Transitional Expressions

Meaning	Expressions
addition	and, furthermore, moreover, too, also, in addition, next, besides, first, second
contrast	although, in contrast, but, conversely, nevertheless, however, on the contrary, on the other hand

Meaning	Expressions
time	later, earlier, when, while, soon, thereafter, meanwhile, whenever, during, now, until now, subsequently
location	nearby, adjacent to, beyond, above, below
comparison	similarly, in the same manner, in like manner, likewise
cause	because, since, on account of, for that reason
illustration	specifically, for instance, for example
effect	therefore, consequently, accordingly, as a result
summation	in summary, in brief, to sum up
conclusion	in conclusion, finally
referring back to an object or idea	this, that, these, those (The pronoun reference must be clear and near the antecedent to avoid a pronoun reference error.)
to replace a noun	Use personal pronouns for coherence to avoid unnecessary redundancies.

Varied syntax is an important component of good writing. A variety of well-written sentences helps maintain the reader's interest in the essay. Writers should use sentences that differ in length and begin with varying words, rather than repeating the same word at the start of each new sentence. It is also important for writers to use a mix of different sentence structures, including simple, complex, compound, and compound-complex sentences.

Teachers should instruct students how to choose words and tone that are appropriate to the task. For instance, a formal essay on an academic topic may benefit from complex sentences and an expansive vocabulary. On the other hand, a first-person essay on a personal topic may use more casual organization and vocabulary. Students should also be instructed to use clear, direct vocabulary and avoid using vague, general words such as *good, bad, very*, or *a lot*. While varied word choice can help improve an essay, it is better to use more familiar vocabulary than to try to impress the reader with unfamiliar words or those that do not fit the context of the essay. **Overwriting** occurs when writers try to imbue their work with inappropriately and awkwardly ornate language or complex, technical terms. Not only might this kind of writing seem disingenuous to the audience, but it will also likely become difficult to follow.

> **HELPFUL HINT**
>
> Transitions between paragraphs can be polished by starting paragraphs with references to ideas mentioned previously in the text or by concluding them with a transition to the next topic, which helps guide the reader from one paragraph to the next.

PRACTICE QUESTIONS

Use the following text to answer questions 3 – 5.

(1) For centuries, artists and philosophers have long debated about the relationship between life and art. (2) While some argue that art is an imitation of life, others believe that, just as often, life ends up imitating art. (3) In no other genre is the impact of art on our real lives more visible than in the realm of science fiction. (4) Great minds of science fiction such as Jules Verne, Gene Roddenberry, H.G. Wells, and Stanley Kubrick have introduced ideas that, though fantastical at the time of their inception, eventually became reality. (5) Many of these artists were dead before they ever saw their ideas come to life.

(6) Some of humanity's biggest accomplishments were achieved first in science fiction. (7) Jules Verne wrote about humanity traveling to the moon over a century before it happened. (8) Scientists Robert H. Goddard and Leo Szilard both credit his work—on liquid-fueled rockets and atomic power, respectively—to the futuristic novels of H.G. Wells. (9) Gene Roddenberry, the creator of *Star Trek*, dreamed up replicators long before 3-D printers were invented.

(10) Jules Verne's work, for example, was the inspiration for both the submarine and the modern-day helicopter. (11) H.G. Wells wrote about automatic doors long before they began to turn up in almost every grocery store in America. (12) Roddenberry's *Star Trek* is even credited as the inspiration for the creation of the mobile phone. (13) Kubrick's HAL from *2001: A Space Odyssey* represents voice control at its finest, long before virtual assistants were installed in all the new smartphone models.

3) In context, which of the following is the best version of the underlined portion of sentence (1), which is reproduced below?

… artists and philosophers have long debated about the relationship between life and art.

- A. … artists and philosophers have examined the facts and debated about the relationship between life and art.
- B. … artists and philosophers have hemmed, hawed, and debated about the relationship between life and art.
- C. … artists and philosophers have debated about the relationship between life and art.
- D. … artists and philosophers have hemmed and hawed about the relationship between life and art.

4) Which of the following introductory phrases should be inserted at the beginning of sentence (6), which is reproduced below?

Some of humanity's biggest accomplishments were achieved first in science fiction.

- A. Therefore,
- B. In fact,
- C. However,
- D. In addition,

5) In context, which of the following would provide the best introduction to the final paragraph?

   A. Transportation was of particular concern to science fiction writers, who dreamed up new ways for humanity to get around the world.

   B. These same authors had other interesting ideas as well.

   C. Sometimes science fiction is so much like life it is incredible.

   D. Many of the ideas life borrows from science fiction have infiltrated our everyday lives and our world to an even greater degree.

RESEARCH RESOURCES

Forming a specific and answerable **research question** provides the focus of the writer's research and is a crucial component of the planning process for students learning how to write research papers or essays. For example, the topic *education* is too broad to result in meaningful research findings. Writers must therefore narrow their topic to *higher education* or, even further, to higher education in the *twenty-first century*. From there, writers must further hone their focus by formulating a specific question to explore: *What are some of the changes that institutions of higher education must address to stay relevant in the twenty-first century?* After formulating a research question, the writer searches for relevant, impactful information from credible sources.

With today's student relying heavily on the internet for information, teachers have the responsibility to not only guide students in the appropriate use of digital resources but also ensure they understand the importance of print resources and how to utilize them. Most importantly, teachers must equip students with the knowledge of how to

- ▸ evaluate the credibility of a text based on its source;
- ▸ evaluate contemporaneity (how up-to-date the research is);
- ▸ determine the purpose of the research.

Print resources may generally be more credible because they go through numerous reviews before arriving in the hands of the researcher. Print resources include books, magazines, newspapers, and journals. **Digital and online resources**, on the other hand, may pose a bigger challenge for young researchers since the internet provides limited—if any—oversight regarding who can post information online or its reliability. Students must therefore be taught to remain particularly aware of inaccuracies and bias when using the internet for research.

Students should be directed toward reliable online sources and how to locate these. Credible sources provide research that

> **HELPFUL HINT**
>
> Less credible online sources include personal blogs, opinion pieces, and online message boards.

is trustworthy because the information has been fact-checked. Such sources include **peer-reviewed journals** (journals that ask other experts to review content before it is published) and websites from reputable institutions such as the World Health Organization or the American Academy of Pediatrics.

It is critical for students to learn the skills needed to evaluate online sources on their own. Some questions they may ask include the following:

- Is the article from a peer-reviewed journal?
  - Most research journals identify themselves as peer-reviewed on their website or in the journal itself.
  - It is recommended to limit library database searches to include only peer-reviewed research.
- Is the article recent?
  - Articles that are over a decade old may contain information that is out of date or that has since been proven inaccurate.
- Is the author trustworthy?
  - Is the author of the article listed?
  - Does the author have academic credentials (such as a PhD) or hold an academic post?
  - Is the author free from bias, or does the author seem to promote a particular political view or personal agenda?

> **HELPFUL HINT**
>
> Primary sources are usually written by people who have directly experienced an event. Secondary sources are written by people who did NOT experience the event themselves.

When conducting research, students should understand the difference between primary and secondary sources. A **primary source** is an unaltered piece of writing that was composed during the time the events being described took place. A **secondary source** might address the same topic as a primary source but provides extra commentary or analysis. For example:

- A book written by a political candidate to inform people about their stand on an issue is a primary source.
- An online article written by a journalist analyzing how that position will affect the election is a secondary source.

PRACTICE QUESTIONS

6) Which of the following sources would NOT be a good choice for an authoritative print source in a research project?

   A. a book published by the NRA that cites statistics from Canada to support a pro-gun agenda
   B. a recent magazine article from *Psychology Today* that reviews mental health assessment tools
   C. a dissertation explaining new research on the use of sentence diagramming with adult learners
   D. a sacred text that discusses the basic tenets of a religion

7) The students in Professor Johnson's class are searching for secondary sources for a paper on the polio vaccine. Which of the following might they consult?

   A. an interview with a person who has been diagnosed with polio
   B. pictures of patients who have received the polio vaccine
   C. a journal article on the rate of polio inoculation in the United States
   D. an interview with a doctor who specializes in the treatment of polio

CITING SOURCES

In discussing the use of reference materials, teachers must also understand and address the topic of **source integration**—how a resource is used effectively without overwhelming the writer's own voice and ideas. Some general guidelines for resource use include the following:

▶ Resources should not be overused or underused.

▶ They should support the writer's ideas appropriately without overshadowing them or replacing them altogether.

▶ Whenever possible, writers should avoid beginning and/or ending paragraphs with cited material; this ensures that the resources are truly integrated and that the ideas that are shaping the paragraphs via the topic sentences are the writer's own.

Sources can be integrated into a research paper in three different ways: by quoting, paraphrasing, or summarizing. A **quotation** is an exact (or near exact) transfer of content and punctuation from a resource into a research paper. Quotations should be less than four lines long and are denoted directly in the text using quotation marks and a parenthetical citation. Sometimes, longer quotes are included if they are especially impactful; such quotes should be offset to signify a significant break from the writer's own words. Quotes are most effective when integrated completely into sentences and paragraphs of a research text, which is why bracket and ellipses rules exist to clarify any sections of a quotation that the writer might have altered in order to lend coherence to the sentence or paragraph.

A **paraphrase** is not simply a synchronistic syllable replacement of words; it involves changing both the wording and the syntax used to express an idea. In other words, when paraphrasing, writers restate a specific piece of information from a source in their own unique voice.

Summaries are similar to paraphrases in that they require authors to use their own voice; however, summaries usually cover much more material. While writers may paraphrase a particular point or idea from an article, for example, they may summarize the article as a whole.

All three types of source integration—quotations, paraphrases, and summaries—require citation according to the appropriate style manual, or guide. Proper **citations** have two parts:

1) The original source must be credited within the document itself (**in-text citation**).
2) The source must then be credited at the end of the document using a reference page, a bibliography page, or a works cited page.

Style manuals function as guidebooks for the documentation of sources within a written document. Some style manuals that apply more narrowly to specific technical fields may be used. For instance, the **Publication Manual of the American Psychological Association (APA)** is used for the fields of education, psychology, and other social sciences. Many word processing programs have tools and references to assist writers in adhering to various writing styles and their citation formats. Numerous websites and applications are also available to assist in the easy formation of accurate citations. The most common style guides are discussed below.

APA in-text citation

The general trend in the early 1900s was to consult the student, an action that had, up to that time, been looked upon as "soft pedagogy" (Tolman, 1902, p. 159).

APA references page

Tolman, A. (1902). The revival of English grammar. *The School Review, 10*(2), 157 – 165.

The **Modern Language Association Style Manual and Guide to Scholarly Publishing (MLA)** is used in the arts, humanities, and literature.

MLA in-text citation

The popularity of fantasy opened up "other worlds" to readers: "He was a faun. And when he saw Lucy he gave such a start of surprise that he dropped all of his parcels" (Lewis 114).

MLA works cited page

Lewis, C.S. The *Chronicles* of *Narnia*. New York: Harper Collins, 1994. Print.

The **Chicago Manual of Style (CMOS or Chicago)** is widely used in the sciences, history, literature, and art.

Chicago in-text citation

The power of the naval forces could not be underestimated. "So great was the force of the big naval guns that surgeons swore they had seen men killed by the wind of a passing shot."[1]

Chicago footnote

1 Toll, Ian W. Six Frigates: *The Epic History of the Founding of the U.S. Navy.* New York: W. W. Norton & Company, 2006.

A Manual for Writers of Research Papers, Theses, and Dissertations by Kate Turabian (Turabian) is used for history and theological studies. Turabian is very similar to Chicago style. The difference between the Chicago and Turabian styles is the largely stand-alone nature of Turabian. Readers of an article written in Chicago style may have to reference other materials to fully understand what they are reading. Readers of an article written in Turabian style will find stand-alone information within the text itself.

Turabian in-text citation

It is difficult to understand Hoekema's "new-self." For example, Hoekema acknowledges the difficulty of differentiating between the objective and subjective parts of sanctification.[25]

Turabian footnote

25 The objective or definitive part of sanctification is that which is finished at salvation. Hoekema explains this in the Reformed view in pages 73 – 74 of the *Five Views on Sanctification.* He terms progressive sanctification as "subjective."

Turabian bibliography

Hoekema, Anthony A. "Reformed Perspective." In *Five Views on Sanctification*, ed. Stanley N. Gundry, 59 – 90. Grand Rapids: Zondervan, 1987.

Electronic sources are those which are primarily accessed online. With the rapid development of electronic communication and publishing, style manuals have had to evolve quickly to accommodate new reference formats: websites, online books, journal articles, DVDs, online magazines and newspapers, interviews, and more. While many style guides have turned away from requiring URLs and other complicated details, some citations still require a DOI (Digital Object Identifier). Writers must therefore consult specific manuals for instructions and details. When citing electronic sources, writers should take note of the following elements:

- ▶ the author(s), compiler(s), or editor(s) of a text, keeping in mind that the authors may be a corporation or group

- ▶ the title of the book, article, website posting, or blog, especially if it differs from the name of the website or the website sponsor

- ▶ the name of the website, often revealed in the URL (www.apa.studies)

- the sponsor of the website or an associated organization, institution, or company

- the date that the electronic source was posted (as in website articles) or published (as in articles from online periodicals)

- the date that the researcher accessed the source

- the format of the source (Note: If a resource is a PDF, it may be because this source is actually a print source; otherwise, online reference materials fall under the web format.)

An example of citing an electronic source with a DOI (Digital Object Identifier) can be found below:

> Kuh, G. (1999). How are we doing? Tracking the quality of the undergraduate experience, 1960s to the present. *The Review of Higher Education, 22*(2), 99 – 120. doi: 10.1353/rhe.1999.0003

When research writers summarize, paraphrase, or quote the ideas or conclusions of others but neglect to credit the original sources, they are committing plagiarism. Whether the result of malice or ignorance, **plagiarism** is a serious offense with serious consequences. Academic, professional, and even legal consequences can arise from the improper and unethical use of another person's work. It is therefore imperative that teachers instruct students on the proper methods for citation.

> **HELPFUL HINT**
>
> When in doubt as to whether information is considered common knowledge, it is always safer to credit a relevant source or consult with a style manual.

One type of information that does not need to be cited, however, is **common knowledge**, which refers to the set of facts and information that is reiterated frequently and assumed to be true among a group or within a culture. In the general public, common knowledge is broad: it is information that the typical person can be expected to know. Within a group of medical professionals, on the other hand, common knowledge takes on a different meaning—one in which a basic understanding of medical terminology is assumed.

PRACTICE QUESTIONS

8) Which of the following would be an effective way to introduce and integrate a source into a research paper?

   A. Some people think "...
   B. This quotation says it well: "...
   C. I don't know how to say this, but this author says it best: "...
   D. Dr. Philip Stern, professor at Iowa State University, concluded after his experiment that "...

9) Which of the following answer options accurately paraphrases the following quotation?

"Eighty-eight percent of the adult learners in the control group scored below the adult learners in the experiment group."

- A. Lots of folks did well in the experiment group.
- B. Eighty-eight percent of the adults in the control group did better than the adults in the experiment group.
- C. Hooray for the experiment group; they did super fantastic!
- D. After the researcher had administered the final test, the control group scored eighty-eight percent worse than the group that received the intervention.

STRATEGIES FOR WRITING INSTRUCTION

Research concerning writing instruction has resulted in a number of empirically tested, outcome-driven strategies that ELA teachers employ to continuously teach and assess their students. Some of the most commonly practiced strategies are described below.

Writing workshop is an approach that integrates instruction, practice, and assessment in a consistent, daily schedule:

▶ Writing workshop time is first signaled by a particular sound, image, announcement, or environmental change.

▶ The teacher then provides a mini-lesson on a particular skill or segment of the writing process (beginning with idea generation and ending with publication and celebration).

▶ Next, students have time to work on their writing independently or in small groups while the teacher circulates to conduct one-on-one and small group conferences.

▶ Finally, students share their work from the day, especially if they have applied knowledge from the mini-lesson.

Writing teachers might also employ models or modeling in their instruction. **Models** are exemplary examples of writing, which the teacher uses to highlight certain qualities or characteristics. Students view and discuss the model and then attempt to apply this knowledge to their own writing. The teacher may also **model** a particular skill by practicing it, along with the thought process, aloud in front of students.

Collaborative writing is especially useful when students—or the entire class—are new to a particular skill or process and may lack confidence. Collaborative writing occurs when partners or small groups of students work together to complete the full writing process or segments of it. This strategy allows students to share ideas and build confidence; it also provides an avenue by which students can practice how to review writing and provide feedback. **Process writing** involves teaching students a clear process for writing and how to use techniques and strategies for completing each part of the process. The writing process typically includes

- planning (brainstorming, outlining, mapping);
- drafting (writing);
- revising (adding and deleting, rewriting, reorganizing);
- editing (editing and proofreading).

Teachers can also use specific activities and exercises to help students develop strong writing skills throughout the writing process. Some of these strategies are discussed below and grouped by their stage in the writing process.

Planning

Data dump is an informal prewriting method. Students write down a topic and then any words that immediately come to mind. For example, a student might write *environmentalism* and then list terms like *climate change, pollution,* and *endangered animals.* After a data dump, students select only the words that most closely pertain to their chosen topic.

In **guided pre-writing,** the class (or a group of students) comes up with ideas and/or a writing structure. The teacher helps by visually projecting ideas or writing them on a board. Mapping, outlining, webbing, and listing are common strategies for guided pre-writing. **RAFT** is a prewriting method that encourages students to consider their purpose, audience, and organization pattern. Students think about the following questions:

- <u>R</u>ole of writer: What perspective will you, as the writer, take?
- <u>A</u>udience: Who will read the piece?
- <u>F</u>ormat: How will you communicate your message (story, essay, drama, and so forth)?
- <u>T</u>opic: What will you write about?

Media or tech-enabled planning involves students watching a video, looking at images, or searching for ideas online. This can be a useful strategy for students who are stuck or who do not have an opinion on an issue or a clear topic to write about.

Drafting

Framed paragraphs, a scaffolding technique, are fill-in-the-blank templates used to help students write paragraphs. For example, an "empty" frame for a persuasive paragraph might look something like this:

> I think that _____. The first reason I think this is because _____. The second reason I think this is because _____. Lastly, I believe that _____. For these reasons _____should_____.

Paragraph or essay hamburgers encourage students to plan a paragraph or essay with the topic sentence or introduction as the top "bun" and the concluding sentence or concluding paragraph as the bottom "bun." The supporting details, or body paragraphs, are the middle parts of the "hamburger."

Shared or interactive writing is a process in which writers are scaffolded by "experts," usually teachers. In **shared writing,** the teacher scribes for the students, who must give explicit direction concerning what to write. This can be an effective method for students who have difficulty with the physical task of writing. In **interactive writing**, students compose the written piece, but the teacher serves as the subject matter expert who facilitates the process. Both shared and interactive writing processes help students see and participate in an effective model for writing, which can give them confidence and strategies to use in independent writing assignments. In both methods, the teacher helps scaffold learning as needed. This might involve the following:

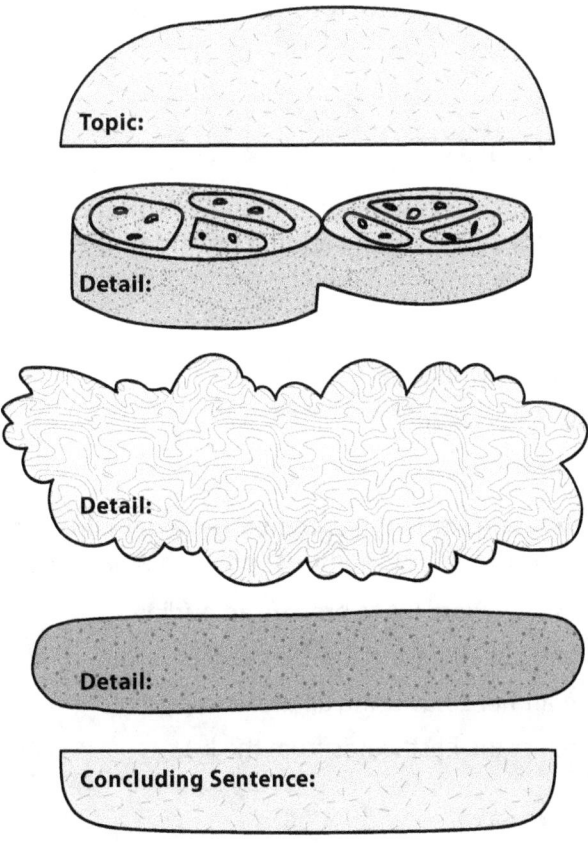

Figure 4.3. Paragraph Hamburger

- asking leading questions ("What should happen after _____?")
- offering ideas for transitions or breaks ("Let's start our next sentence with 'Additionally,'")
- providing more explicit instruction to reinforce concepts ("Now, we need to add supporting details. What supporting details can we add?")

Revision and Editing

Modeling or think-alouds can be used with a sample piece, which can be authored by the teacher or a student (with the student's permission and name removed as requested), and should involve whole-class input. The piece can be projected on a screen and edited through a "track changes" feature in a word-processing program or even copied onto a transparency and written on. Teachers can encourage input from the class and model strategies to revise writing, such as reading aloud, identifying and refining thesis and topic sentences, and so on. This process is helpful since it allows students to participate in and experience the revision and editing process.

Conferencing or peer review can also be used after first modeling the process and providing guidelines to students. Research proves that the most successful writing conferences are structured and occur when students have a clear idea of what type of feedback they should provide and how to give feedback in a constructive way. **Self-assessment** should also be taught as part of the revision process: students can be given a checklist or rubric from which to assess their own drafts and make necessary revisions.

PRACTICE QUESTIONS

10) Ms. Johnson wants to teach a simple introduction to the process of revising for coherence by adding transitional words and phrases. Which instructional method would be the MOST appropriate?

    A. collaborative writing
    B. writing workshop
    C. process writing
    D. modeling

11) A ninth-grade student has completed a data dump pre-writing exercise with the topic of "autonomous vehicles." What should she do next?

    A. use her word list to prepare an outline
    B. think of synonyms for each of the words
    C. draft her essay using all the words
    D. select the best words from the list

Answer Key

1) **C** — A school-wide literary journal is an effective way to publish and distribute creative writing in a high school.

2) **C** — A thesis statement presents the writer's main argument.

3) **C** — This version of the sentence is the clearest, most concise option for communicating this idea.

4) **B** — *In fact* can be used correctly in this instance to draw attention to interesting information that builds on the previous sentence.

5) **D** — This option provides a brief but interesting overview of the information to come.

6) **A** — A book written by a special interest group may be biased.

7) **C** — Option C is the only secondary source listed; options A, B, and D all contain firsthand information.

8) **D** — The example in Option D includes a specific authoritative source, an active verb, and integrates the quotation into the text.

9) **D** — This paraphrase is a rewording and a syntactical alteration by the author of the paper; it is both accurate and academic.

10) **D** — When introducing a new skill, teachers should first model it for students in order to illustrate confidence and eliminate confusion.

11) **D** — After a data dump, students can refine their list by circling the most closely associated words or crossing out unrelated words.

Speaking, Listening, and Viewing

ORAL LANGUAGE DEVELOPMENT

Oral (spoken) **language** and the development of reading skills are entwined in children from a young age. Students who understand the role of oral language in communication and how to produce and "consume" oral language will have a head start in learning how to read and write well.

Students who have a large spoken vocabulary will be far more likely to identify words in text. Those who have heard and participated in complex conversations and discussions will make connections and activate background knowledge as they read. Further, oral language and an understanding of its structures are critical components in phonics instruction, which relies on the connection between written and spoken language.

Students should be expected to use oral language to think critically and communicate their thoughts. This process relies on both **receptive oral language,** the ability to understand what is being said, and **expressive oral language**, the ability to use language to communicate ideas appropriately. For older students, techniques for developing oral language skills for critical thinking and creative expression include

- oral discussion or critiques of literature or expository texts;
- reciprocal teaching (students become the teachers and guide a small-group reading activity);
- "book club" or book discussion activities in large or small groups;
- oral discussions with peers on current events or issues that require critical reflection;
- persuasive speeches or presentations;
- plays or dramatic performances;

- writing and reading a piece of creative writing aloud;
- impromptu dialogues or role-plays.

Nuances related to each student's home language (dialect, register, and so forth) should be respected in assessing and building oral language skills. While educators might have certain notions of the "right" or "wrong" way to speak, such a distinction does not exist organically. Speech may not be well matched for a particular setting or audience, but it is not "wrong." In assessing and building oral language proficiency, such a distinction should be kept in mind. An overemphasis on speaking English "correctly" without consideration for unique registers and dialects removes language from its pragmatic context and fails to account for the broad diversity within the spectrum of spoken English.

> **HELPFUL HINT**
>
> **Pragmatics** refers to the way we use language (oral or otherwise) for a practical purpose.

PRACTICE QUESTION

1) A ninth-grade English teacher asks a reading specialist how to incorporate oral language for critical thinking into his unit on Shakespeare's *Romeo and Juliet*. Which instructional strategy is the reading specialist MOST likely to recommend?

    A. filling out a graphic organizer before, during, and after reading the play
    B. reading the play aloud with dramatic inflection
    C. holding a class-wide debate on whose fault the tragedy really was
    D. encouraging students to use fix-it-up strategies as they orally read the tragedy

ORAL COMMUNICATION ACTIVITIES

Oral communication exercises in the classroom come in a variety of forms: they may be formal or informal and may occur one-on-one, in small groups, or as a whole class. In planning an oral communication exercise, teachers make numerous considerations to ensure that the work is productive and purposeful. Effective teachers must

- know the objective of the lesson;
- choose an appropriate and relevant topic for discussion;
- decide on a format;
- define appropriate student behavior;
- determine accountability measures.

The objectives of oral communication exercises are often twofold in an ELA classroom:

1) They are usually conducted in the context of a broader unit and therefore may be centered on a particular reading objective (for example) and used in part to assess a student's grasp of a particular reading assignment, chapter, or unit.

2) They address oral communication objectives such as fluency, coherence, and clarity.

First and foremost, the **topic** of an oral communication exercise must stem from the lesson objective. The exercise must also be age appropriate and have some relevance to students' lives or the world at large. In choosing a suitable topic, effective teachers consider the emotional and intellectual development of their students, the required background knowledge for discussion of the topic, and the objectives that they hope to see their students master. After choosing a topic, the teacher should decide what **form** the exercise will take:

▶ Will students give a speech, presentation, or participate in a debate or discussion?

▶ Will they interact with only one other student, a group of students, or the whole class?

▶ Will communication flow in all directions or just in one?

▶ How directly will the teacher be involved?

Teachers may assign a **debate** in order to test students' abilities to both speak intelligently on topics they have researched and defend their positions with evidence. Debates also assess the students' ability to handle stress and respond to academic arguments with composure. A debate can take many specific forms in the classroom; in general terms, it requires students to take a side on a particular issue and provide evidence for their reasoning. Depending on the teacher's objective, debates can be one-on-one, in a small group, or with the whole class.

A teacher may assign a **speech** in order to evaluate students' formal public speaking abilities and observe their fluency and ability to communicate emotionally with an audience. A speech requires students—usually one at a time—to stand in front of a group and speak on a particular topic. The speech format is fairly versatile: speeches can range in length and formality depending on purpose, audience, and topic—all of which can vary widely. More information on the delivery of speeches is provided below.

Discussions may also be assigned in order to assess students' informal speaking and listening abilities as well as their verbal reasoning skills. In general, discussions allow participants to gain a deeper understanding of a specific topic or text but otherwise are varied in format. Effective teachers might consider the objective and the culture of their classrooms when choosing discussion formats.

For less complex topics, **one-on-one** discussions may be assigned in the form of **think-pair-shares,** in which students have the opportunity to first share briefly with a partner before sharing their responses with the whole class. Think-pair-shares are appropriate when everyone in the class can comment on a topic without much prompting or when every student is expected to have a response. This method is also helpful in new classes, where students are still getting to know each other and might feel more comfortable testing their responses out on just one classmate first.

> ### IMPORTANT WORKS
>
> *The Gettysburg Address*
> **Speaker:** Abraham Lincoln
> **Date:** November 19, 1863
> **Summary:** Lincoln delivered this brief address at the dedication of the national cemetery at Gettysburg, Pennsylvania—the site of the Civil War's bloodiest battle. He begins by reminding listeners of the Declaration of Independence and the ideals upon which the US was founded. He explains that a cemetery in this location is fitting but that the men who died there—not the people gathered on that day—are the ones consecrating the ground. He encourages listeners to persevere in the war effort so that these men will not have died in vain. He closes with another reference to the nation's founding and calls for the establishment of "a new birth of freedom" and a government that continues to be by, for, and of the people.
> **Themes and Rhetorical Strategies:** appeal to patriotism and history, death and rebirth, struggle

Small group discussions also allow for a level of safety since students are asked to share on a smaller, more intimate scale. They are therefore particularly helpful in classes where students may be unwilling to speak in front of a large group. In classes that are large or particularly vocal, small groups can also be helpful for getting every student engaged and giving everyone an opportunity to share. Teachers might discover, however, that small group discussions can be difficult to manage since they must monitor many discussions at once. For this reason, accountability measures are especially important in small groups.

Whole class discussions, especially those conducted in classrooms that are safe and productive, can be especially useful for taking on broad, complex ideas that require many perspectives. Larger thematic questions related to the human condition, for example, can be explored in more dimensions when a larger number of perspectives and opinions comes together. The **Socratic seminar** format, in which a leader (the teacher or a student, depending on the classroom culture) prompts discussion by asking questions and allowing the class to share, respond to, and build upon one another's ideas, is especially effective and engaging.

Once the objective, topic, and format of the oral exercise have been determined, teachers should consider and define **appropriate student behavior** for the exercise and share this information with students. Some teachers may prefer to involve their students when defining these parameters by asking them what they consider appropriate discussion or debate behavior. Some particulars to consider include the following:

- Are students required to participate?
- If so, when and how much?
- Is there a maximum that students can contribute?
- Will they be required to use academic language during the exercise?
- What is appropriate behavior in response to a disagreement?
- Can students talk over each other? If not, how will that be managed?
- What is an effective or meaningful contribution?
- How will the group respond to comments that are inappropriate, irrelevant, or distracting?

In addition to defining appropriate behavior for students, teachers should also be prepared to share with students how they will be held accountable for their contributions to a discussion or debate. Accountability may take the form of a rubric-based grade, a follow-up written assignment, or a related project that requires tangible output.

PRACTICE QUESTIONS

2) Which of the following would be the MOST appropriate assignment for assessing how well students can integrate evidence into an argument in order to prove a point?

   A. a speech
   B. a debate
   C. a think-pair-share
   D. a Socratic seminar

3) Mr. Green's class will soon be completing a discussion on F. Scott Fitzgerald's use of figurative language in *The Great Gatsby*. Which of the following is NOT an effective way for Mr. Green to hold his students accountable for this activity?

   A. He can require students to participate a minimum number of times during the discussion and track the students' contributions.
   B. He can have students complete a series of multiple choice questions covering figurative language in *The Great Gatsby*.
   C. He can assign students to write an independent response after the debate to discuss any moments that stood out or changed their minds about something.
   D. He can ask students to complete a prediscussion list of questions to turn in on discussion day.

EFFECTIVE SPEECHES AND PRESENTATIONS

In preparation for the professional world, today's students must know not only how to write a speech but also how to deliver a speech or presentation effectively. As with writing, purpose and audience are the two most important considerations in writing and giving a speech. Other elements of effective presentations include but are not limited to

- tone;
- bias;
- conciseness;
- clarity;
- visuals.

Audiences pick up on nuances of **tone** almost as quickly as they recognize a lack of eye contact or the use of unusual body language. Indeed, *how* the speaker delivers the message of a speech may be just as—if not far more—important than *what is said*. Before delivering a speech, speakers should rehearse extensively in order to ensure that they are employing the appropriate gradations of emotional tone:

- genuine or sarcastic
- casual or formal
- cold or warm
- sincere or insincere
- familiar or distant
- kind or harsh
- judgmental or nonjudgmental
- passionate or disinterested

Conciseness in writing and speech delivery means much more than shortness; it involves the conscious ridding of superfluous wording, including clichés, fillers, and verbose sentence structure. A speech writer who is editing for conciseness cuts words not purely for the sake of shortening a speech but for the sake of choosing language that is clear and simple and that the audience will easily be able to understand.

> **HELPFUL HINT**
>
> **Semantics** refers to the meaning of words. English dictionaries are the resources containing the semantics of the English language.

Writers must sometimes continuously play with words until conciseness and clarity result. They may move, replace, cut, and add words until their sentence says exactly—no more and no less than—what they want it to say. While this practice can be tedious, the process of revising for clarity and conciseness allows writers to apply their knowledge of word nuances to achieve a satisfying end.

When it comes to speeches and presentations, **visual aids** can be extremely helpful and allow writers or speakers to emphasize elements throughout their presentation. If used incorrectly, however, visual aids can be a detriment to a good presentation. Some recommendations about the use of visual aids appear in Table 5.1.

Table 5.1. Visual Aids

Recommendation for Visual Aids	Explanation
Do not let the visual aid overpower the presenter.	The speaker should be the focus throughout most of a presentation, not the visual aid. A PowerPoint presentation, for example, can be distracting if too much detail or animation is included on the slides.
Do not stand in front of a visual aid.	Most importantly, the speaker must avoid blocking the visual aid for any portion of the audience. With a projection, standing in front of the visual aid creates a silhouette effect. Both are distracting and prevent the audience from experiencing the effect of the presentation as a whole.
Practicing with the visual is important.	Sometimes good intentions with a powerful visual aid go awry because the speaker has not sufficiently practiced with it or has not considered possible mishaps. Especially when using technology, speakers should be familiar with troubleshooting methods and have an alternative approach ready should their technology fail.
Look at the audience despite the visual aid.	Nervous speakers might depend on the visual aid for support and look more at the visual aid than at the audience. This signals a lack of confidence and prevents speakers from fully connecting with their audience.
Make sure the room is appropriate for the visual aid.	Sometimes visual aids will be too large or too small for the location or audience, either of which can be distracting. Speakers should therefore be familiar with the presentation space and location of their audience.
Make sure the visual aid has a clear purpose.	A visual aid—especially a chart, graph, or image—will only be effective if the audience understands its purpose. If a visual aid is never explained or referred to throughout the course of a presentation, it can probably be removed.

continued on next page

Table 5.1. Visual Aids (continued)

Recommendation for Visual Aids	Explanation
Keep it simple.	When it comes to visual aids, simpler is often better. Endless bullet points, too many sensory images, or too much information can overwhelm an audience and cause viewers to lose interest in the visual, the speaker, or both.

Developing students' skills with **presentation software** (Microsoft PowerPoint or Prezi, for example) is also part of an effective ELA teacher's curriculum. Presentation software, slides, images, videos, movie clips, charts, graphs, songs, sound clips—or any combination of these and other technologies—can be integrated into presentations to support and emphasize the speaker's main points. Teachers must understand these technologies not only so that they can apply them in their classrooms but also so that they can instruct students how to use these technologies most effectively—a skill that will continue to benefit them throughout their educational careers and into the workplace.

PRACTICE QUESTION

4) What are some guidelines that a speaker should follow when using a PowerPoint for a speech about city planning?

    A. simply sit down by the PowerPoint with a clicker in hand, and let the slides speak for themselves

    B. fill the PowerPoint with graphics, animation, word art, music, and surprise sounds to entertain the audience since the message will be most effective with a flashy and exciting design

    C. use the PowerPoint as a visual tool with carefully chosen, dynamic images, incorporated at specifically chosen moments

    D. create several slides with bullet points and then add transitions that cause the words to bounce in and out of each slide to keep the attention of the audience

HELPFUL HINT

Teachers should make the same considerations as speakers do concerning visual aids by embracing them and learning how to apply and execute them appropriately in the context of a lesson. Like presentations, lessons can be derailed by faulty, unnecessary, or otherwise distracting visual aids.

NONVERBAL COMMUNICATION SKILLS

Developing students' nonverbal communication skills is equally as important as developing their oral language skills. **Nonverbal communication** refers to any way communication occurs outside of speech. Examples of nonverbal communication are

▶ **paralinguistics** (tone, loudness, inflection, and pitch);

- facial expression;
- gestures;
- body language/posture;
- proximity;
- eye contact.

IMPORTANT WORKS

Martin Luther King Jr's "I Have a Dream" speech
Speaker: Martin Luther King Jr.
Date: August 28, 1963
Summary: King gave this famous speech at the March on Washington, a protest against racial discrimination. He begins by referencing the unfulfilled promises of the Emancipation Proclamation as African Americans still do not have the same freedoms as White Americans. He then calls for continued nonviolence in protests and to unite with White allies. He encourages listeners to continue to fight for justice when they return to their homes throughout the nation. King then explains his dream for the future of the country in which all people will be judged by their character and not their skin color. He ends with a call for people to work together so that America, founded on the principle of freedom for all, can truly be a nation of freedom for all.
Themes and Rhetorical Strategies: anaphora, or repetition of "I have a dream"; nonviolent resistance; hope; freedom; the fight against racism

Each of the instructional activities discussed in this chapter can also focus on nonverbal communication skills as part of overall oral communication. Additionally, activities such as having students play charades or act out a "silent" movie can show them how even nonverbal communication has an impact.

Students can focus on paralinguistics by practicing speaking for an audience and then reviewing an audio or video recording of themselves. They can also analyze audio or video recordings of famous speeches for tone and inflection or other nonverbal communication, such as gestures or eye contact. Eye contact and body language are integral in effective speech delivery. A speaker who makes **eye contact** with the audience, for example, will likely be perceived as more honest, genuine, and accessible than a speaker who looks above the audience or does not meet the eyes of the general audience at all.

Effective speakers also make an emotional connection with their audiences by meeting the gaze of as many members as possible throughout the course of a speech. Additionally, effective speakers consider **body language** and seek to present themselves as calm and confident in their gestures and posture.

Educators should not judge culturally nuanced means of nonverbal communication as incorrect or correct but should focus instead on what is most appropriate for a given situation. Students should also be made aware that nonverbal communication varies based on locale, and different cultures have different norms or standards for gestures, eye contact, volume of voice, and so on.

> PRACTICE QUESTION
>
> 5) A high school English class watches and then discusses a video of a TED Talk. They agree that they enjoyed the speaker's presentation but that his tone seemed too angry, which obscured the message. Which aspect of oral communication did they critique?
>   A. paralinguistics
>   B. prosody
>   C. morphology
>   D. semantics

LISTENING SKILLS

Listening skills can be slower to develop than language skills, especially among younger children. A popular technique with younger students is **whole body listening.** This strategy gives students explicit instruction in how to listen with their entire body:

- Eyes should be on the speaker.
- Ears should be listening.
- Mouth should be quiet.
- Hands should be in the lap or away from others.
- Feet should be still.
- Body should be pointed toward the speaker.
- Brain should be thinking about what it is hearing.
- Heart should be considerate of others.

Active listening is the process of fully concentrating on speakers and their messages; it is focused and empathetic. Students should be taught the following aspects of active listening:

- Focusing: Students practice keeping their attention on the person who is speaking.
- Positive nonverbal cues: Students demonstrate interest by looking at the speaker and using appropriate facial expressions and body language.
- Allowing speaker to finish uninterrupted: Students wait for a speaker to finish and concentrate on the message before formulating a response.

▶ Nonjudgment: Students listen and respond with respect for the speaker's views and feelings. They agree or disagree using methods that maintain respect within the whole group.

▶ Paraphrasing: Students verify understanding by restating the speaker's main points concisely and in different words.

PRACTICE QUESTION

6) Which of the following quotes is a demonstration of active listening?
   - A. "If I understand correctly, you think the class needs more time on this project."
   - B. "I think you meant to say that you need more time to finish this project."
   - C. "You didn't say how much more time you would need to finish."
   - D. "There's no way I can let you have more time to finish this project."

Media Literacy

Types of Media

Media has rapidly evolved over the last century. **Radio** was once the primary media outlet for news and entertainment. Although it is still used, its popularity has been supplanted by other types of media as technology has become more advanced. **Movies** became popular with the invention of film in the early twentieth century. **Television** became a mainstream product in the 1950s, bringing broadcast media into people's homes. The **internet,** which became popular in the late 1990s and early 2000s, quickly led to the creation of many new genres of media, including podcasts, social media, and video/music streaming. Today, media is usually categorized into four types:

▶ **print media** (physical magazines and newspapers)

▶ **broadcast media** (film, TV, and radio)

▶ **outdoor media** (billboards and banners)

▶ **digital media** (websites, social media, and podcasts)

Media—regardless of the type—will always influence society, and some of these influences are negative. For example, media can allow people to easily disseminate false information and spread harmful stereotypes or biases. It can also desensitize people to violence and suffering through repeated exposure.

However, not all of the impacts of media are negative. The internet can spread information much more quickly than other types of media and allows people from all over the world to collaborate. It also gives people access to news that was not traditionally available through radio, newspapers, or television. The internet can be particularly useful to populations who historically have not been able to produce traditional broadcast media.

Media is also the primary way through which businesses advertise their products or services. **Advertisements** are found in all types of media, and are often the main way that media content is funded. For example, ads may be shown before or during streaming videos, and news websites usually sell ad space to raise revenue.

In many types of media, the line between ads and content can become blurred. This is especially true for digital media, wherein **sponsored content**—ads paid for by businesses—might be integrated into social media accounts or websites. As part of media literacy, students should be taught how to identify ads or sponsored content in all types of media.

IMPORTANT WORKS

"Day of Infamy" speech
Speaker: Franklin Delano Roosevelt
Date: December 8, 1941
Summary: The speech was delivered the day after the Japanese attacked Pearl Harbor. Roosevelt begins by explaining that the attack was unprovoked and that Japan and the US were in peaceful negotiations at the time. However, because of the distance between Hawaii and Japan, he concludes that the attack had been planned for some time, which he sees as an intentional deception. FDR explains that many lives were lost and that Japanese forces subsequently attacked Malaya, Hong Kong, Guam, the Philippines, Wake Island, and Midway Island. He says that the US will use force to defend itself and that it will be victorious. He concludes by formally asking Congress to declare war on Japan.
Themes and Rhetorical Strategies: appeal to emotion, anger, betrayal, war

PRACTICE QUESTION

7) Which of the following is an example of broadcast media?
   A. a social media account
   B. a newspaper
   C. a radio show
   D. a billboard

ANALYZING MEDIA

HELPFUL HINT

Advances in technology have allowed businesses to target very specific groups of customers. As part of a media literacy program, students can study how their online habits shape the types of ads they see.

Media literacy is the ability to find and effectively analyze media content. All types of media—from magazines to movies to podcasts—can be analyzed in much the same way as traditional texts. Students should learn to assess both the content and context of the media they consume. Important aspects of media analysis include

- the message or main idea of the content;
- the intent or purpose of the people who produce the content;
- the effect the media has on the audience;
- the techniques used to produce this effect.

Teachers often begin the process of analyzing media by explaining to students that no media is completely neutral: every piece has a **message**. Students should be able to identify the key information communicated in a piece of media and understand how it builds the message.

To place media's message in the proper context, students must look for the **intent** of its producers—who made this piece of media and why? Every piece of media has a purpose. Like informational texts, media can inform, persuade, or entertain.

To identify the purpose of a piece of media, students should first identify the person or organization behind it. Knowing this information allows students to assess the producer's **bias** so they can evaluate the strength of the content. Asking the following types of questions can help students determine bias:

> **HELPFUL HINT**
>
> As part of a media literacy program, students should learn how advertising drives content in digital media. Often, the intent of producers is simply to attract viewers and raise ad revenue.

- Is the producer a person or company with a vested interest in the subject matter?
- Are the producers experts in their fields, or do they have any professional qualifications?
- Is the producer a magazine or news organization with a known political bias?
- How are the producers funded and how might this affect their biases?
- Once the creator is identified, the intent of the media can be analyzed. For example, if a notable scientific study is being covered in media, the intent of the media creator will determine how that study is presented.
- The university that did the study may promote it with an upbeat article on its website.
- A news site may drive traffic to its site by focusing on sensationalized aspects of the study.
- A company may use the study to advertise their own products.
- Social media accounts may use the study to promote a specific political agenda.

Media can have many different **effects** on the consumer and can affect an individual's knowledge, attitudes, beliefs, and behaviors. These effects might change the way an individual thinks or behaves or reinforce existing beliefs and behaviors.

There is debate in media studies about the strength of media effects. Older theories, such as the **direct effect theory**, were based on the belief that people passively consumed media and were strongly and directly affected by it. Newer theories, some of which are discussed below, emphasize that people's relationship to media is more complex:

▸ **agenda-setting theory:** The media has the ability to influence which topics people think are important but has less effect on what people think about those topics.

▸ **framing theory:** A person's understanding of the world is influenced by how media presents topics, including the media's use of language and chosen point of view.

▸ **cultivation theory:** People who consume media, particularly TV, are likely to perceive the world as it is depicted in media.

▸ **uses and gratifications theory:** People actively seek out and consume media to meet specific needs.

▸ **spiral of silence:** Media shapes which views are perceived as "minority positions," and people who perceive themselves as holding minority views are less likely to voice these.

HELPFUL HINT

Propaganda is communication designed to influence public opinion, often through partial truths—or even total falsehoods. Students should learn to identify propaganda and become familiar with the various logical fallacies it often uses.

To help students develop skills in evaluating various types of media, they should be exposed to multiple sources of information and learn how to compare and contrast them. For example, an informational article or podcast could be compared to a documentary film on the same topic. Similarly, advertisements across various platforms like radio, print, and film—both past and present—could be compared to identify techniques used and how those impact the viewer, reader, or listener.

Along with comparing media representations of various topics, students should be taught to confirm facts from a variety of sources and spot examples of media messages that contain lies or claims that cannot be verified through other sources. Again, the availability of technology can be a help. For example, in the past, the public often had to rely on word of mouth to confirm the claims of advertisers about a product or service; now, online reviews can reveal much and help consumers make informed purchases.

Speaking, Listening, and Viewing   147

PRACTICE QUESTIONS

8) Students are watching a news clip in which a police officer talks about the destruction of a homeless camp. The teacher then asks the students how the story would be different if the presenter interviewed a homeless person. What media effect is this lesson highlighting?

   A. agenda-setting theory
   B. spiral of silence
   C. framing theory
   D. uses and gratifications theory

9) A middle school teacher wants to design an activity to help students confirm the accuracy of information in a YouTube video about a historical topic. Which activity is MOST appropriate?

   A. having students compare the information in the video to multiple photographs covering the same topic
   B. assigning students the task of creating their own videos on the same topic
   C. encouraging students to use the information in the video to create a multimedia presentation on the same topic
   D. asking students to compare the information in the video with that in multiple print sources

Creating Media

The use of varied media often makes a message clearer and more engaging. Many national and state standards require students to work on media projects such as presentations, videos, posters, charts, graphs, and audio recordings. Often, these types of projects promote curricular integration as students use media skills to analyze and present information across content areas.

Teachers should help students learn to create high-quality and engaging multimedia projects. Effective presentations should

- contain an appropriate balance of media elements;
- use sound, images, and video aligned with the overall message of the presentation;
- offer opportunities for audience participation, if possible;
- be aligned with the project purpose and audience.

Students should strive to use media in their work for a specific purpose—often to elaborate on a point or help the audience visualize something. The use of media elements as "decoration" or "fluff" is generally not a best practice. Students should therefore be taught to recognize and evaluate effective presentations, both those they make themselves and those made by others. Rubrics customized for specific types of media can be very helpful for both teacher and student evaluation of media.

With the increased use of media comes more responsibility. Students should use appropriate online etiquette and must learn to navigate fair use issues in the digital space.

Students creating and posting media must follow basic **netiquette** protocols, meaning they should use a communication style appropriate to the online environment. Most schools and districts have netiquette policies, which might include

- keeping the people behind digital communications in mind at all times;
- remembering that nothing posted online is private or temporary;
- using an appropriate tone for the audience;
- maintaining the privacy and confidentiality of others;
- avoiding the use of all caps, emojis, or slang.

HELPFUL HINT

Types of art that CAN be copyrighted include written works, paintings, photographs, musical compositions, movies, and sound recordings. Things that CANNOT be copyrighted include recipes/formulas, ideas, slogans, and common knowledge.

When creating media, students must also learn how to correctly use and cite media sources. Copyright is the legal ownership of a work of art. **Copyrighted** works can only be reproduced or repurposed under specific conditions.

Fair use refers to the legal use of **copyrighted** work without the permissions of the rights-holder in certain circumstances. Fair use doctrine follows four main guidelines:

1) Purpose and character of use: Education and nonprofit use of copyrighted works is usually permitted. Works that are transformative—meaning they add something substantially new—are also usually able to use copyrighted materials.
2) Nature of the work: Personal, creative works of art are less likely to be considered for fair use.
3) Amount and substantiality of the work: Using small portions of copyrighted works is often permitted.
4) Effect of the use on the market for copyrighted material: Reproduction of copyrighted materials that substantially affects the ability of the original creators to market their products is not allowed.

Classroom use of copyrighted content often falls under fair use guidelines because it is for educational purposes; however, the principles of fair use must still be considered. For example, it may be appropriate for students to use properly cited images in a slide presentation given to the class. It would not, however, be appropriate for students to use those copyrighted images on their personal websites without the copyright-holder's permission. In these cases, the material has two different purposes: one is a limited educational setting; the other is the broad online dissemination of someone else's work.

Of course, not all media is copyrighted. Work that is in the **public domain** is free for use because its copyright has expired, was forfeited, or never existed. Students can be directed to sites that offer photos and images in the public domain.

Additionally, some work falls under a **Creative Commons** license. Creative Commons (CC) is a nonprofit that helps content creators designate how their work may be used. All CC content must be attributed to its creator. Further, there are multiple types of CC licenses that dictate how the work may be used. Some require that the content only be used for noncommercial purposes or that it only be reused if the new work will also fall under a Creative Commons license.

> **IMPORTANT WORKS**
>
> *"On Women's Right to Vote"*
> (Title variations include: "Women's Right to the Suffrage" and "Is it a Crime to Vote?")
> **Speaker:** Susan B. Anthony
> **Date:** 1873
> **Summary:** After being arrested, tried, and found guilty of voting in the 1872 presidential election, Anthony was required to pay a $100 fine. This speech explains why she refused to pay and why she believed she was innocent. She begins by quoting the preamble of the Constitution, explaining that "we the people" refers to all people—not just men. She argues that denying women voting rights denies the consent of the governed and creates a "hateful oligarchy of sex." Anthony concludes by explaining that women are citizens and thus have the right to consent to be governed. Therefore, any law that discriminates against women and African Americans is void because it denies their rights as American citizens.
> **Themes and Rhetorical Strategies:** appeal to logic rooted in the Constitution, citizenship, equality, personhood, discrimination

Students and teachers should also be aware of liability before using images or videos featuring other students. Schools and districts will typically have a media release policy and associated forms that parents must sign. Without such documentation, photos and videos of students should not be posted on any online platforms, including class websites or social media pages.

> **PRACTICE QUESTION**
>
> 10) A high school teacher assigns an activity wherein student groups create a website highlighting the life and work of a well-known author of the past. What should the teacher advise students before they begin?
>
>   A. They can use any type of media on the site because it is for educational purposes and thus falls under fair use.
>
>   B. They should avoid the use of any images on their website because of the risk of copyright infringement.
>
>   C. They should seek out image sources that are in the public domain or that have certain types of CC licenses.
>
>   D. They can use most types of media on the site but should provide links to the original sources for proper citation.

Answer Key

1)	C	In a class-wide debate, students have to think about the play critically, form an opinion, and then express that opinion orally.
2)	B	A debate requires students to research a particular topic and gather evidence to support their position on it.
3)	B	This approach is not effective because it would not necessitate participation in the discussion; the students could likely answer these questions without engaging with the discussion.
4)	C	Visuals should be used sparingly and purposefully.
5)	A	Paralinguistics refers to the parts of speaking outside of the words themselves, such as tone, loudness, inflection, and pitch.
6)	A	This quote demonstrates active listening because the listener is paraphrasing the message to clarify understanding.
7)	C	Broadcast media is transmitted to the public in real time and includes film, TV, and radio.
8)	C	The teacher is highlighting the framing theory by showing students how the media's chosen point of view affects how the story is perceived.
9)	D	Information in various media can best be confirmed by comparing it to other sources.
10)	C	Public domain and certain types of Creative Commons (CC) licenses allow use without permission.

6

Assessment and Instruction

Assessment

Effective assessment is the cornerstone of good teaching. Teachers who cannot properly assess their students can neither meaningfully adjust instruction nor provide useful feedback to encourage student growth. Knowledge of different kinds of assessments and their applications is therefore necessary for educators in order to provide the best instruction possible for their students.

Different methods of assessment have different applications, and each method has unique strengths and flaws. Understanding these qualities will allow educators to choose effective assessment techniques that are truly aligned with the objectives they are hoping to assess.

Standardized Assessment

There are numerous **standardized** published assessment instruments which have standardized questions or criteria and are administered in a consistent manner. These assessments fall into two categories: norm-referenced and criterion-referenced.

Norm-referenced assessments measure an individual student against a group of other test takers, typically those of the same age or grade level. Results are reported in a percentile ranking or as grade-equivalent scores.

A **percentile** is a score that shows where a student ranks in comparison to ninety-nine other students. For example, a percentile of 81 means that the student in question has performed equal to or outperformed eighty-one out of the other ninety-nine students who took the same test. **Grade-equivalent scores** provide results as a grade level, meaning that the student's performance is equal to the median performance corresponding to other students of a certain grade level.

Achievement tests, such as the Iowa Test of Basic Skills (ITBS) and the Peabody Individual Achievement Test, measure which skills a student has mastered. These often fall under categories like reading and mathematics, are generally multiple choice, and require test takers to answer a standardized set of questions.

Another type of norm-referenced assessment is the aptitude test. Like achievement tests, **aptitude tests** measure learned abilities, such as mathematics and verbal reasoning. They also help predict the course of future learning. The SAT and ACT are two very common aptitude tests used to predict the probability of a student's success in a college environment.

Criterion-referenced tests measure an individual's performance as it relates to a predetermined benchmark or criteria. These tests are generally used to measure a student's progress toward meeting certain objectives; they do not compare test takers to one another but rather compare student knowledge against the set criteria. Criterion-referenced tests include everything from annual state tests to those created by teachers or educational publishers to assess mastery of learning objectives.

One new incarnation of the criterion-referenced test used by many states is **standards-referenced testing or standards-based assessment.** These tests measure a student's performance against certain content standards as defined by each grade level and subject and are typically scored in categories such as basic, proficient, and advanced or unsatisfactory, satisfactory, and advanced. Most annual state accountability tests, including the State of Texas Assessments of Academic Readiness (STAAR) and the Partnership for Assessment of Readiness for College and Careers (PARCC) are standards-based, criterion-referenced tests.

PRACTICE QUESTION

1) When planning lessons, a teacher wants to use test scores as a starting point in order to improve vocabulary knowledge among students. Which assessment results would be most appropriate for her to reference?

    A. Iowa Test of Basic Skills
    B. annual state accountability test
    C. SAT scores
    D. results from running records

Types of Assessment

Formal assessments refer to test results that are reported in either a percentile or percentage format. Examples include

- standardized tests;
- chapter or unit tests
- end-of-course exams.

Informal assessments evaluate students outside of the traditional written test format and help give a more complete picture of ongoing progress. In certain situations, particularly when students experience stress in high-stakes testing scenarios, informal assessments include

- observation;
- portfolios;
- projects;
- presentations;
- oral checks.

Whether formal or informal, assessments can also be either formative or summative. **Formative assessment** refers to the ongoing monitoring of student progress toward learning objectives. These are often informal assessments in which teachers seek more information to streamline instruction. However, they can be more formal, such as a short quiz over the day's material. Formative assessments do not significantly impact a student's course grade or chances of promotion to the next grade.

Summative assessment is designed to evaluate student learning after the end of a defined unit of study. It compares student knowledge to the initial learning objectives that were addressed throughout the unit of study. It may be formal or informal but often takes the form of a unit test, midterm, final exam, or final paper or project. Summative assessments are generally considered high stakes because they carry high point values. They are often critical to a student's overall grade, ability to pass a course, or promotion to the next grade.

> **HELPFUL HINT**
>
> Formative assessments are used while students are *forming* their knowledge. Summative assessments are used to add up all of student learning into one lump *sum*.

A middle ground between a formative assessment and a summative assessment is the **benchmark assessment,** which is more formal than a formative assessment but not as high stakes as standardized summative assessments. Benchmark assessments are sometimes called interim assessments or predictive assessments. They track student progress and determine the degree to which students are on track to perform well on future summative assessments.

Authentic assessment measures the student's ability to use knowledge in a direct, relevant, and real-world way. In an authentic literacy assessment, students apply reading and writing skills in a pragmatic or practical

> **HELPFUL HINT**
>
> **Diagnostic assessments** are used to determine what students already know. They are given by many teachers at the beginning of the school year or before each unit of study to calibrate the level of instruction and track progress over time.

way. For example, an authentic assessment of the skills needed to write for a formal audience might include having high school students work on writing a resume or a profile on a professional networking platform.

Teachers may also ask other students to participate in the assessment process. This is known as **peer assessment**—the evaluation of student work by peers. If students receive appropriate guidance and practice, peer assessment can be used effectively in many secondary classrooms. In a peer assessment, students are given a rubric or list of criteria upon which to assess another student's work. They are then asked to offer specific feedback for improvement. This process can help students who are unsure of how to revise or edit their work since they are given clear and actionable suggestions.

> **HELPFUL HINT**
>
> While most peer assessments will not result in a formal grade, they can be invaluable in helping students revise their work before submitting it for grading.

Multi-perspective assessments are also used during cooperative learning activities. In these types of assessments, peers, the individual student, and teachers all collaborate to assess learning outcomes. This method can be helpful when parts of a group project occur both in and out of the classroom. In a multi-perspective assessment, the teacher may weigh input from different assessors differently when computing the total overall grade. For example:

- The teacher evaluation of the finished project may count for 75 percent of the grade.
- The peer assessment of group members might count for another 10 percent of the grade
- Finally, the student's self-assessment could count for the remaining 15 percent of the grade.

PRACTICE QUESTIONS

2) A teacher wants to assess student retainment of skills at the end of a small-group intervention aimed at vocabulary acquisition. Which method of assessment should be used?

　A. a norm-referenced assessment
　B. ask students to write down three new words they learned
　C. have students take a 25-question multiple-choice test
　D. a standardized achievement test

3) A tenth-grade English teacher wants to create an authentic assessment to evaluate students' skills with writing in coherent paragraphs. Which assignment would be best?

　A. directing students to give a presentation to the class on something they know how to do well

B. asking students to analyze the way paragraphs are used in a newspaper article
C. assigning students to write the draft of an email they will eventually send to someone
D. having students use a graphic organizer to formulate their thoughts into paragraphs before writing an essay

ASSESSING WRITING SKILLS

Assessing writing skills in a holistic, constructive way is a unique challenge for secondary ELA teachers, who must find ways to both assign scores to students' work and provide feedback to help them improve their writing skills. The goal for all of the assessment tools and response strategies discussed in this section is to provide students with useful feedback about their writing.

Teachers who plan to provide a traditional, numbered score (usually zero to one hundred) on a writing assignment may want to include a rubric. **Rubrics** are assessment tools that teachers use to objectively assign scores to projects or assignments whose merits are difficult to quantify, especially writing assignments. Well-designed rubrics make grading guidelines clear for both the teacher and the students so that confusion and subjectivity are eliminated as much as possible. Two commonly used rubrics are the holistic rubric and the analytical rubric.

Holistic rubrics provide a grade based on the overall effectiveness of the product. For example, holistic rubrics might assign a score based on the overall effectiveness of an argumentative essay.

Analytic rubrics break the product down so that points are assigned by component part. For example, an analytic rubric for an argumentative essay would separately score the thesis, evidence, organization, and grammar to produce an overall score.

In addition to rubrics, writing teachers employ a variety of other assessment techniques to provide students with useful, timely feedback. Providing feedback is a skill in itself and a responsibility that can be shared between the teacher and students. Effective teachers understand the value of constructive criticism and prioritize the need for regular writing feedback.

> **HELPFUL HINT**
>
> Analytic rubrics are more useful than holistic rubrics when it comes to highlighting areas of improvement for students. Holistic rubrics are more efficient as grading tools and more reflective of how writing is assessed and evaluated in the real world.

> **HELPFUL HINT**
>
> Useful feedback consists neither of falsified praise nor crushing criticism; it is an authentic celebration of strengths and a suggested pathway for improvement in the future.

Sometimes, teachers may hold **writing conferences**—either as needed or at particular times throughout the year—to provide the feedback themselves. The purpose of a writing conference is to help students improve their writing skills by highlighting individual strengths and homing in on the areas most in need of improvement. **Portfolios** are also useful tools for assessment since they allow both the teacher and student to track and observe growth over time.

PRACTICE QUESTION

4) A ninth-grade English teacher is grading a nonfiction writing assignment using a holistic rubric. Which of the following should the teacher NOT do?

   A. mark the number of points deducted for each criteria not met by the student
   B. ensure that each student receives credit for effort
   C. consider how well the student addressed the writing prompt
   D. assign each student a grade based on the overall quality of the individual works

INSTRUCTION PLANNING

STANDARDS AND OBJECTIVES

To ensure their students are getting the most they can from language and content lessons, effective teachers organize their instruction around the content and objectives. To do this successfully, teachers must have clearly defined content and language objectives that fall under the umbrella of the academic standards.

Content area standards identify what students are supposed to learn throughout a given time period in a specific subject area. Each content area has its own set of standards, which can be yearly or unit standards. Both yearly and unit standards are intended to guide instruction and clearly define goals for students' learning. Content area learning is intended to be aligned to these standards to ensure that all students are learning the same material:

- Yearly standards identify goals and expectations for students' annual learning. The Common Core State Standards are one example.

- Unit standards are created by the teacher and clearly lay out expectations for students' achievement in a single unit.

Content objectives identify what students should be able to do at the end of a content area lesson and are related to the key concepts being taught; they are usually the same for all students in the classroom. Content objectives should be clearly stated so that students can understand them without explanation. They should have measurable goals that are achievable in the given time for the lesson. One example of a well-written content objective is, "Students will explain three contributions made by George Washington that improved the lives of people living in the United States." This objective clearly states what students should be able to do at the end of the lesson and can be measured in a number of ways.

Language objectives describe how students will learn and/or demonstrate their mastery of materials by reading, writing, speaking, or listening. A strongly written language objective provides a precise look at the expectations for students' learning. For example, the objective "Students will make predictions about the events in the short story using future tense and conditional verbs," states what students will be expected to do, what materials they will use, and what kind of language they will use. Each element of the objective is clear and measurable. Effective language objectives meet several criteria:

- They are formed using the tasks of the content area lesson.
- They emphasize the communicative skills of speaking and writing without neglecting the importance of listening and reading.
- They use active verbs to name targeted functions.
- They specify the target language that students will need to complete the task.
- They focus on language that is suitable for students' use in other contexts.

PRACTICE QUESTION

5) Which of the following statements is a clearly written language objective?
   A. Students will learn about the life of Mark Twain.
   B. Students will write a summary of their science lab.
   C. Students will identify and define the adjectives used in character description.
   D. Students will listen to two pianists' interpretations of Beethoven's Fifth Symphony.

Promoting Mental Development of Students

While students can develop many mental skills on their own, teachers can promote this development through lessons and activities that are aimed at increasing understanding and awareness of cognitive and metacognitive strategies. These differ from the skills students use inherently since they require some thought to determine which strategy should be used.

Cognitive strategies help students remember and organize both content and language learning information. Deliberate instruction in cognitive strategies can help all students become more successful in their learning. For example, it is common to skim the title, headings, and pictures for information when reading. This strategy is taught to children as they are learning to read and often becomes habitual with good readers; it develops into a skill. Skimming assists students in anticipating what they are about to read and aids them in making predictions.

Another common practice is grouping information. When presented with large amounts of material, it is helpful to separate the information into chunks that relate to one another. Some teachers show students how to do this with graphic organizers, diagrams, or outlines.

Regardless of the strategy, direct instruction in cognitive practices aids students in understanding the content and linguistics they are learning. The five types of cognitive strategies used to aid students in their learning are discussed in Table 6.1.

Table 6.1. The Five Types of Cognitive Strategies

Strategy	Purpose	Steps
Comprehension strategies	• help students understand and remember content	• broken into subcategories: monitoring, using text structure, summarizing, elaborating, and explaining • When explicitly taught to use these strategies, students can more easily retain and comprehend information.
Writing strategies	• help students complete unstructured tasks • teach students the importance of planning in order to conceive and organize ideas	• After they plan their work, students begin generating a piece. • After the initial draft, revisions and edits are made before presenting the final product. • Students who complete all of the steps in writing strategies are more likely to create comprehensive, well-composed pieces.
Problem-solving strategies	• help students see ways in which they can achieve a specific goal	• Students are presented with a problem and must identify steps to solve it. • The most popular steps involve teaching students to understand the problem, then to develop a plan for solving it. • Students then carry out the plan and look back to see what can be learned from their process and solution.
Reasoning strategies	• help students determine what they believe to be true or false, correct or incorrect	• Successful reasoning involves the creation of arguments and counterarguments, fair evaluation of evidence, and consideration of sources.

Strategy	Purpose	Steps
Self-regulation strategies	• help students monitor their behaviors	• Students who master self-regulation are capable of successful self-monitoring and evaluations, time management, and goal setting. • These skills aid them in their learning endeavors by contributing to their metacognitive processes and focus.

Metacognitive strategies are those that focus on thinking about thinking. They involve knowledge of one's own thinking processes, one's own knowledge itself, and the limitations of that knowledge. Metacognition is not an inherent process; students must be taught how to analyze their knowledge in order to successfully plan, monitor, evaluate, and revise their thinking to engage in various learning environments and subjects.

Metacognitive strategies teach students how to identify their prior knowledge of a topic, recognize what they don't know about something, and what it is that they still need to learn. They help students plan their learning, self-regulate, and choose appropriate cognitive strategies to aid them as they study new material. Direct instruction in metacognitive strategies can lead to increases in learning; implementing these strategies results in success and self-sufficiency.

Table 6.2. Metacognitive Strategies

Strategy	Description
Identifying what is known and what is not	• Students need to recognize their prior learning and then move forward in determining what they don't know, what they need clarification on, and what knowledge has stuck with them.
Planning	• Estimating the time a task will take, organizing materials, scheduling group or individual work time, and determining procedures for completing a task all require planning. • Students should assume responsibility for these components of planning in order to become self-directed. • Criteria for evaluating their planning process should be established and taught as students proceed through an activity.

continued on next page

Table 6.2. Metacognitive Strategies (continued)

Strategy	Description
Keeping a thought journal	• Logging their own thoughts and ideas can help students reflect upon their thinking and understanding of a topic and understand any difficulties they are struggling with as they work through a problem or process.
Talking about thinking	• This process must be modeled for students. • Teachers should think aloud during problem-solving and planning activities to show students what this process looks like. • This will enable students to understand what it means to talk about their thinking and demonstrate the benefits of doing it.
Self-evaluating	• This process should be modeled for students. • Providing students with checklists or one-on-one conferences can help them develop the skills necessary for determining their own understanding. • As students come to recognize how to implement strategies and where they are most useful, they will develop the ability to evaluate their use of them for success as well as their understanding.
Debriefing	• Activities that focus on closure help students develop awareness of the strategies they implemented, as well as where their successes and areas of improvement are. • It helps students recognize the cross-curricular uses of many of the strategies they employ.

Activating students' prior knowledge can help them make connections between what they already know and what they are going to learn. In order to activate students' prior knowledge, there are several strategies that teachers can use to encourage students to think about what they already know:

Introduce vocabulary before content: Presenting students with words and learning about them prior to being expected to apply them will allow students to gain comfort and familiarity with new words and demonstrate their understanding and practice of words they already knew. This strategy can also help students recall familiar topics within given content.

Use graphic organizers, outlines, and diagrams: Helping students visualize content can aid them in recall. By creating a visual aid to organize information, students are able to see the material in the topic and potentially recall prior learning.

Brainstorm ideas about the topic or content: Students are able to toss out ideas they have and make connections with what they already know when completing brainstorming activities. It may help students generate connections that they did not know existed.

Ask questions about the content or topic and things related to it: This kind of exercise can help students use vocabulary they already know and prepare them to use what they are going to learn in communicative ways.

PRACTICE QUESTION

6) Which of the following strategies is NOT intended to aid students in activating prior knowledge?

   A. asking questions about the content
   B. introducing vocabulary before content
   C. using graphic organizers, diagrams, and outlines
   D. listening to an expert speaker discuss the content

CULTURAL CONSIDERATIONS

In today's language classrooms, diversity extends both to language itself and to the learning process as a whole. Teachers must understand variations in language usage across time and place and be able to instruct students to not only use language in the context of their own culture and community but also to understand and adapt to the unique characteristics of language usage in other places and times as well.

Teachers must simultaneously be conscious of how language and culture are impacting their own classrooms and be able to employ diversified, research-based instructional techniques to meet the diverse needs of their students. To do this, it is imperative that teachers make a number of considerations to ensure that the needs of each student are being met.

It is imperative that teachers create a safe learning environment: Students must be taught what is appropriate and inappropriate in an academic environment, especially with regard to academic risk-taking and personal identity. Students should never be shamed (by the teacher or by other students) for making mistakes or sharing their opinions; this can prevent them from making efforts altogether.

An inclusive environment should also be created by involving numerous, varied voices in classroom discussions, offering reading material by authors of different backgrounds, and having students write and speak about their own experiences. Together, these tactics can breed acceptance in the classroom. Ultimately, all students need to feel that they, their perspectives, and their opinions and ideas are valuable in the classroom environment.

Teachers must also understand the identities of their students—both as individuals and as a group—in order to practice instruction that is responsive to their needs and circumstances. For example, a class that consists of college-bound seniors may have a different set of needs from a class of seniors who plan to graduate and move immediately into the workforce. A classroom with a high immigrant population will have different needs from a classroom of students who speak English as their first language.

PRACTICE QUESTION

7) A ninth-grade English teacher uses class discussion on controversial issues as a prewriting technique to help students form opinions for persuasive essay topics. The teacher notices that the discussion gets very heated, and several students appear to have hurt feelings. What changes should the teacher make in his classroom?

   A. avoid oral discussion of controversial issues since ninth graders lack the socio-emotional competence to understand diverse perspectives

   B. conduct prewriting activities individually and not cooperatively since diverse perspectives obscure the intended focus

   C. set class-wide ground rules about appropriate language and interactions with peers who express diverse or contradictory perspectives

   D. focus the discussion on topics that students have no fixed opinion about so that perspectives will be less diverse and discussions less heated

English Language Learners

Second-Language Acquisition

Researchers agree that **second language acquisition** occurs through a series of stages, much like first language acquisition. Learners must pass through each of the five stages on their way to proficiency, though the time spent in each stage varies from person to person.

Table 6.3. Stages of Second Language Acquisition

Stage	Description
Preproduction (silent period)	• Learners may have upward of 500 words in their receptive vocabulary, but they refrain from speaking.
	• They will listen and may copy words down.
	• They can respond to visual cues such as pictures and gestures.
Early production	• Learners achieve a 1,000-word receptive and active vocabulary.
	• Learners can produce single-word and two- to three-word phrases and respond to questions and statements.
Speech emergence	• Learners have a vocabulary of about 3,000 words.
	• They are able to chunk simple words and phrases into sentences that may or may not be grammatically correct.

Stage	Description
Intermediate fluency	• Learners have a vocabulary of about 6,000 words.
	• They can speak in more complex sentences and catch and correct many of their errors.
	• Learners may communicate well but have large gaps in their vocabulary, grammar, and syntax skills.
Advanced fluency	• Learners achieve cognitive language proficiency in their learned language.
	• They demonstrate near-native ability and use complex, multi-phrase and multi-clause sentences to convey their ideas.

As language learners progress through levels of study, they usually develop an interlanguage to aid them in their progression. **Interlanguage** is the learner's current understanding of the language they are learning. It is a rule-based system that develops over time and tends to blend aspects of the learner's first language with those of the second.

When language learners stop progressing and the development of their interlanguage stops, their understanding can become fossilized. **Fossilization** is the point in second-language acquisition when a learner's growth freezes, and further linguistic development becomes highly unlikely.

HELPFUL HINT

Sometimes students will repeat what they hear in a process called **parroting**. This can help them build their receptive vocabulary, but it should not be mistaken for producing language.

PRACTICE QUESTION

8) Lucia enjoys listening to songs in English. She memorizes the choruses and sings them to herself. She notes words she does not recognize and integrates phrases from the songs into her everyday language practice. When asked about the songs, Lucia responds in single words and short phrases but struggles to compose complete sentences. What stage of second-language acquisition might Lucia be in?

    A. preproduction
    B. early production
    C. speech emergence
    D. intermediate fluency

FIRST-LANGUAGE INFLUENCE ON SECOND LANGUAGE LEARNING

Students' native languages will always impact their learning of English. The influences will occur in all parts of language learning, from grammatical understanding to vocabulary acquisition to syntactical awareness. English language learners (ELLs) are bound to transfer their understanding of their first language to their studies of English to make sense of what they are learning.

Transfer occurs when a student applies knowledge of a first language to another language and can be both positive and negative. **Positive transfer** occurs when students find similarities between their native language and English and use those similarities to help them learn. For example, a Spanish-speaking student may recognize the English verb *to comprehend* because it looks like the Spanish verb *comprender* ("to understand"). Visually similar words like these are **cognates.**

Words that look similar but have different meanings are **false cognates.** For example, the Spanish verb *comprar* means "to buy," not "to compare." Students who are learning a new language should understand that both cognates and false cognates exist.

> **HELPFUL HINT**
>
> A student's ability to recognize cognates and use them as a tool for understanding a second language is called **cognate awareness.**

Negative transfer, also called interference, occurs when students incorrectly apply rules from their native language to their learning of English. For example, a Spanish-speaking student may place an adjective after a noun ("the house red") because of the noun-adjective structure in Spanish. However, in English the adjective comes before the noun ("the red house").

Code-switching is also frequent among language learners. Students mix in words from their first language with the language they are learning. This often happens when they have forgotten a term or do not know how to express themselves in the second language. For example, a Spanish-speaking student who is looking for the bathroom and cannot recall a vocabulary word might ask, "Where is the *baño?*" This type of linguistic back-and-forth is very common with bilingual and multilingual individuals.

Finally, students' **accents** will impact their learning and pronunciation of English. Speakers will often substitute the sounds of their first language for ones they think are the same in English. For example, some Spanish speakers may pronounce the /v/ sound like the English *b*. Additionally, stresses and intonations of words can be carried over from first languages, and both of these speech patterns can change the meanings of English words. For example, the meanings of the words *read* and *read* can lead to an unclear message.

> **PRACTICE QUESTION**
>
> 9) Jamie has just moved from Mexico to Texas, where his mother enrolled him in an ESOL class. A few weeks in, Jamie is still reluctant to speak because he mixes in words from his first language with the English he is learning. Which linguistic behavior is Jamie demonstrating?
>
> A. code-switching
> B. cognate awareness
> C. difficulty with accent
> D. language interference

INSTRUCTION OF ENGLISH LANGUAGE LEARNERS

Like all students, ELLs need developmentally appropriate systematic instruction to build content knowledge and English proficiency. While students are working to master content-specific standards, they will also be working to master **English Language Proficiency (ELP) standards.** Such standards may be created by the state or by the WIDA Consortium (a group of state and government agencies that uses a shared set of ELPs). These standards aim to help students develop language proficiencies related to language arts, mathematics, science, social studies, and the social and instructional language of the school environment.

Within a broader framework of overarching ELPs, educators should create language objectives for ELLs that correspond with each lesson's focus. In schools with a large population of English language learners, some classes may be sheltered. **Sheltered** classes focus on the content area and English language learning, with an emphasis on developing language objectives in conjunction with content area proficiency.

> **HELPFUL HINT**
>
> Some schools use bilingual education to transition to solely English instruction. Other schools use full English immersion with ESOL services through co-teaching, pull-out services, or sheltered or specialized classes.

However, if ELL students are taught in the general education setting, content area teachers will need to embed English learning objectives in their lessons. They will also need to modify lessons and assessments to meet the needs of all learners. Lesson modification and assessment strategies are provided in Table 6.4.

Table 6.4. Lesson Modification and Assessment Strategies for English Language Learners

Lesson Modification Strategies	Assessment Strategies
using picture dictionaries or electronic translators	• giving students a word bank or other explicit prompting
eliminating portions of assignments or assessments students may not have background knowledge of	• allowing a test to be read aloud or completed orally in its entirety
using peer tutors or collaborative learning strategies that build on each student's strengths	• giving written assessments with simplified language
using multimedia or visual elements to aid in understanding	• administering assessments in smaller portions
preteaching core vocabulary or vocabulary scaffolding, such as digital texts with click-through definitions	• allowing students to use a dictionary or translating device on tests and/or allowing for extra or unlimited time

continued on next page

Table 6.4. Lesson Modification and Assessment Strategies for English Language Learners (cont.)

Lesson Modification Strategies	Assessment Strategies
limiting teacher talk and, when used, speaking slowly and avoiding colloquialisms	• not penalizing for spelling or grammar errors (as appropriate)
verifying that instructions are understood before students begin a task	• using informal assessment measures, such as observational records or oral assessments whenever possible
providing both a print and oral version of instructions	
using manipulatives or authentic learning situations whenever possible	
providing copies of lecture notes or allowing audio recording	

Reading and English/language arts teachers are in a slightly different position from content area teachers: they must teach basic literacy skills along with the foundations of English as a language students might not be familiar with. Their focus will be on best practices in reading instruction with an emphasis on the needs of English language learners.

Phonemic Awareness: English phonemes are distinct and should be taught explicitly, particularly for sounds that do not exist in the student's native language. However, sounds that are present and already known in the student's native language can be transferred rapidly. In this case, instruction in phonemes should focus on those that differ from the student's first language.

Systematic Phonics Instruction: As with all learners, systematic phonics instruction is effective with students whose first language is not English. Decoding through phonics is a two-step process:

- Teachers must give ELLs the tools to sound out words.
- These students must be able to make meaning of the words based on their oral language vocabulary, which should be developed in tandem.

Automatic word recognition (sight reading) can also be very helpful for ELLs since it can speed up reading rate and sometimes prevent difficulties that are encountered when words deviate from standard phonetic structures.

Fluency in reading follows oral language fluency; however, ELLs may have trouble with strategies like reading aloud in front of others. Students may lack confidence and focus on mistakes instead of the growth they've achieved over time. Oral reading practice with English language learners should be carefully orchestrated, making use of a trusted peer whenever possible.

Vocabulary instruction for ELLs will vary considerably from that of their native-speaking classmates. English language learners will need instruction in idioms and basic "connector words" like *because, and*, and so on. They will also need explicit and direct instruction in the vocabulary of the classroom. This includes words frequently used in giving instructions, words associated with subject area, high-frequency words used in speech and texts, and all vocabulary necessary to understand a text. Whenever possible, vocabulary should be taught explicitly and backed up with images or objects.

Comprehension must be carefully scaffolded in a variety of ways. Teachers should provide as much background knowledge as possible to students who are unfamiliar with aspects of American culture. Like developing readers, ELLs are better able to comprehend text with low complexity; such texts should be used to build comprehension skills. Graphic organizers, visual aids, and films or multimedia elements to promote comprehension may also be helpful.

Cultural sensitivity describes an awareness of cultural differences. While cultural sensitivity is important for all students, it is especially relevant for English language learners, who may be unfamiliar with elements of American culture that many people take for granted. Assumptions about religious beliefs, dietary preferences, clothing choices, family structures, and so on should be avoided. Teachers should select a variety of texts and curricular resources to promote an understanding of diverse cultural perspectives. While many publishers now promote multicultural awareness, teachers should consider curricular resources that also include diverse authorial voices.

> **HELPFUL HINT**
>
> In 1970, only one in five children with disabilities attended US schools; in fact, many states at that time had laws excluding students with certain disabilities from school.

PRACTICE QUESTION

10) A reading specialist is helping a high school teacher make her unit on *Romeo and Juliet* more accessible to English language learners. Which is the BEST suggestion for the reading specialist to make?

    A. provide an alternate dramatic text on a different topic for ELL students to read
    B. encourage ELL students to use context clues as they read the play to identify new vocabulary
    C. preteach important roots and affixes to ELL students to aid in their decoding of new words in the play
    D. give ELL students a list of words used frequently in the play with their definitions

Reading Difficulties and Disabilities

Legal Issues Related to Reading Disabilities

Today's special education landscape has been shaped by federal legislation over the last fifty years. Before federal legislation mandating school access, many individuals with disabilities were institutionalized rather than given opportunities for education. In institutions, systemic neglect and abuse were common. In the 1960s, alongside other civil rights movements, the disability rights movement raised public awareness of the treatment of individuals with disabilities. The federal government responded with legislation supporting educational opportunities for people with disabilities.

Table 6.5. Federal Special Education Acts

Act	Description
Elementary and Secondary Education Act (ESEA) 1965	• seeks to improve student academic achievement through supplementary educational services and increased educational research and training • provides financial assistance to schools servicing a high percentage of students from low-income families (Title I funding)
Rehabilitation Act of 1973	• ensures all students with disabilities a right to public education
Section 504 of the Rehabilitation Act	• prohibits programs that receive federal financial assistance from discriminating on the basis of disability • requires that public schools provide students with disabilities a comparable education to those without disabilities • allows for students with disabilities to receive related services, accommodations, and modifications to ensure equal access to education
Education for All Handicapped Children Act (EHA or P.L. 94-142) 1975	• ensures that students with disabilities can access any accommodations, modifications, related services, and specially designed instruction needed to make adequate educational progress in a public school setting
Americans with Disabilities Act (ADA) 1990	• prohibits discrimination on the basis of disability in the workplace and all public places • provides another layer of legal protection for the right of students with disabilities to have equal access to public education
Individuals with Disabilities Education Act (IDEA)	discussed in detail in Table 6.6

Act	Description
No Child Left Behind (NCLB) 2001	• sought to improve the academic performance of all students through increased accountability for results, emphasizing research-based instruction, and ensuring such instruction is delivered by highly qualified teachers (HQT)

Act	Description
Every Student Succeeds Act (ESSA) 2015	• replaced NCLB • rolls back many of the federal education requirements, giving power back to the states • states required to create accountability plans, track state-set accountability goals, and incorporate accountability systems

Congress reauthorized EHA as the **Individuals with Disabilities Education Act (IDEA)** in 1990 and again with amendments in 1997 and 2004. Part B of IDEA provides for services for students between the ages of three and twenty-one, while Part C provides for early intervention services for students from birth to three years old and their families. Since its original authorization, IDEA has operated under six foundational principles as described in Table 6.6.

Table 6.6. The Six Foundational Principles of the Individuals with Disabilities Education Act (IDEA)

Principle	Description
Free Appropriate Public Education (FAPE):	• FAPE maintains that students with disabilities have a right to an education at no additional cost to parents.
Appropriate and nondiscriminatory evaluation	• Evaluations must be completed by a team of trained professionals such as teachers or school psychologists, and should include information from parents. • Evaluations should address all areas of concern, be nondiscriminatory, and completed in a timely manner; reevaluations must occur a minimum of every three years.
Individualized Education Program (IEP):	• This is a legal document developed by the IEP team (parents, general educators, special educators, administrators, related service providers) that reports present levels of performance, annual goals and objectives, accommodations, modifications, related services, and specially designed instruction to help students make adequate educational progress.

continued on next page

Table 6.6. The Six Foundational Principles of the Individuals with Disabilities Education Act (IDEA) (continued)

Principle	Description
Least Restrictive Environment (LRE):	• Students with disabilities must be provided supports with nondisabled peers to the maximum extent appropriate for them to make educational progress.
Parent and teacher participation	• Parents must have a shared role in all special education decisions, including IEP reviews, evaluation, and placement decisions.
Procedural safeguards	• Parents must receive written notice of procedural safeguards, parent and student rights, meetings, and all educational decisions. • Parents may take due process measures in the event of a disagreement between the parent and a school district.

The most recent authorization of IDEA is the **2004 Individuals with Disabilities Education Improvement Act.** IDEA 2004 expands procedures for identifying students with learning disabilities to include identification through response to intervention. IDEA 2004 also includes several changes to align with NCLB. If students with disabilities do not qualify for services under IDEA, they may still receive support through a 504 plan. The specifics of each plan are discussed in Table 6.7.

Table 6.7. IEP Versus Section 504 Plan

	IEP	**Section 504 Plan**
Law	Individuals with Disabilities Education Act (IDEA)	• Section 504 of the Rehabilitation Act of 1973
Department	Department of Education	• Office of Civil Rights
Eligibility	a disability as defined in IDEA that impacts educational performance	• a disability that impacts a major life function
Included	specialized education services, accommodations, modifications, related services	• accommodations • modifications • related services
Age	0 – 21 years	• no age limits
Location	schools through grade 12	• schools through grade 12 • college • work

> **PRACTICE QUESTION**
>
> 11) Which of the following would NOT be a service provided to a student under a 504 plan?
>
>   A. occupational therapy
>   B. testing accommodations
>   C. extra transition time between classes
>   D. specially designed instruction

Characteristics of Reading Difficulties and Disabilities

Students progress toward full literacy at different rates. Those who do not meet or are at risk of not meeting grade-level expectations have reading *difficulties*, which are different from reading *disabilities*. Students with **reading difficulties** are falling behind grade-level expectations in reading but do not qualify for special education services under the category of a specific learning disability (SLD). Reading difficulties fall into three categories:

1. **Specific word-reading difficulties (SWD)** describe when students have trouble reading or decoding individual words. Students may also have below-average fluency and comprehension levels because they struggle to decode on the word level; however, when presented with texts they are able to decode, these students may have strong reading comprehension skills.

2. **Specific reading comprehension difficulties (SRCD)** are experienced by students who can decode on a basic level but lack the vocabulary knowledge or inferencing skills necessary to fully comprehend texts.

3. **Mixed reading difficulties (MRD)** describe when students have deficits in both decoding and comprehension.

Reading disabilities are formally diagnosed learning disabilities. Students with reading disabilities will typically qualify for special education services and are served through an IEP. Reading disabilities also fall into three categories:

> **HELPFUL HINT**
>
> Least restrictive environment emphasizes placement in the general education classroom with as many supplemental aides and services as possible.

1. **Phonological deficits** occur when students struggle with word recognition due to weak phonological processing. Students with phonological deficits face a range of challenges, including trouble with letter-sound correspondence, sounding out words, and spelling. Seventy to 80 percent of students with a reading-related learning disability have phonological deficits, which are usually described by the term dyslexia, sometimes called **language-based learning disability (LBLD)**.

2. **Processing speed/orthographic processing deficits** occur when students do not read quickly or accurately. Orthographic coding differs from phonological coding in that it does not rely solely on letter-sound correspondence and knowledge to decode but rather on memory (of letters, groups of letters, or entire words). This type of deficit is typically milder than a phonological deficit and may be co-occurring or distinct from a phonological deficit. There is some debate as to whether this type of deficit is a subtype of dyslexia or a distinct disability.

3. **Specific comprehension deficits** describe challenges with vocabulary, language learning, and abstract reasoning. Comprehension deficits might co-occur with phonological or processing deficits as well as with other conditions, particularly autism spectrum disorder (ASD). This type of deficit is also referred to as **hyperlexia** because word recognition skills are average or even advanced.

Students who qualify for special education services under another category (such as intellectual disability, speech and language impairment, or developmental disability) may have other disabilities that cause reading difficulties. Their IEP may therefore list reading-related modifications and accommodations even though they have not been diagnosed with a specific learning disability.

> **DID YOU KNOW?**
>
> Dyslexia is a very common SLD thought to affect at least 15 percent of the global population.

PRACTICE QUESTION

12) Specific comprehension deficits often co-occur in students diagnosed with which of the following?

   A. dyspraxia
   B. dysgraphia
   C. autism spectrum disorder (ASD)
   D. emotional or behavioral disorders (EBD)

INSTRUCTING STUDENTS WITH READING DIFFICULTIES AND DISABILITIES

Students with reading difficulties and disabilities that impact reading performance need explicit, systematic, direct instruction. Instruction must also be based on each student's needs as revealed through assessment and data collection. If instruction is not targeted in this way, it may be ineffective and/or increase student frustration.

Instructional strategies and intervention techniques for students with reading difficulties and disabilities are generally provided to either increase word identification or decoding on the word level or increase overall comprehension. Specific strategies and interventions are discussed below.

Scaffolding refers to the supports used by teachers (or sometimes peers) during classroom activities. Scaffolds should be built into all lessons per the Universal Design for Learning (UDL), which states that all students should be able to learn from the same curriculum.

Shaping refers to providing incremental reinforcers and is helpful in instructing students with reading difficulties and disabilities. For example, as students progress by memorizing more grade-level high-frequency words, they should receive frequent, positive feedback from educators. This feedback is important for students who struggle with reading since they may not receive the consistent positive reinforcers, such as high grades or praise from peers, that other students who excel academically typically receive.

Students with reading difficulties on the comprehension level benefit most from instruction and interventions that help them develop metacognition to self-assess understanding and apply strategies to integrate information and synthesize it with existing knowledge. Such strategies include semantic mapping or other visual organizers, reciprocal teaching (see Chapters 1 and 5), and the PQ4R method.

In the **PQ4R method**—an extension of the SQ3R method (see chapter 1)—students preview the reading material, generate questions, and read to answer the questions. They then reflect on what they have read, recite or retell from memory what they have read, and review the material for any missed information.

In addition to the instructional strategies above, students with disabilities that impact reading, such as dyslexia, can benefit from certain accommodations. **Accommodations** are changes to materials or instructional methodologies that allow all students to learn the same material as their peers. Material and instructional accommodations include those listed in Table 6.8.

Table 6.8. Material and Instructional Accommodations

Material Accommodations	Instructional Accommodations
underlining or highlighting the key words in directions	• clarifying directions through oral repetition • providing a written version of directions
chunking assignments or presenting them in smaller increments	• implementing daily routines to clarify expectations
using a glossary or list of key vocabulary terms	• providing visual aids whenever possible
using chapter-by-chapter, page-by-page, or even paragraph-by-paragraph reading guides	• encouraging the use of mnemonic devices
using assistive technology	• providing students a hard copy of notes

continued on next page

Table 6.8. Material and Instructional Accommodations (continued)

Material Accommodations	Instructional Accommodations
audio recordings or books on tape	• implementing frequent review and reinforcement activities at the end of each lesson
e-readers or tablets	• reviewing previously learned concepts at the beginning of a new lesson
text-to-speech software	• creating opportunities for additional or extended practice
	• using peer learning strategies

At times, students with reading disabilities will also need modifications to what they are expected to learn. **Modifications** are usually listed on the student's IEP and may include a reduced number of questions or items on assessments, different grading criteria, and so on. ELA teachers may collaborate with special education teachers to develop and monitor accommodations and modifications for students with learning disabilities that impact reading performance.

PRACTICE QUESTION

13) A tenth-grade English teacher wants to help one of her students who has dyslexia and is very frustrated and overwhelmed by the assigned novel the class is reading. Which of the following would be MOST appropriate?

   A. have the student read the CliffsNotes version of the novel instead of the novel

   B. encourage the student to read at least fifty to one hundred pages each day

   C. give the student an audio recording of the book to aid in comprehension

   D. read the entire novel aloud in class, asking a different student to read orally each day

Answer Key

1) **B** — Most annual state accountability tests are standards-based assessments that are criterion-referenced based on state standards. These results would help the teacher align her lessons with both her students' needs and her state's standards.

2) **B** — This is a short, informal assessment that gives the teacher the needed data about what has been retained from the session.

3) **C** — This assignment is an authentic assessment because students will actually send the email to someone, so the assessment has a real-world application. It also allows the teacher to assess the students' use of paragraphs.

4) **A** — Holistic rubrics do not attach point values to specific criteria; instead, a single score is given based on the criteria laid out in the rubric for each score range.

5) **C** — This objective is clear, measurable, transferable to other contexts, and indicates the target language for students' use.

6) **D** — Listening to an expert speaker discuss a topic may be beneficial to students' understanding of the material, but it will not activate their prior knowledge.

7) **C** — Rules such as "always focus comments on the argument, not the person," and "use the most respectful language possible when expressing disagreement" can help students conduct these discussions more effectively with fewer hurt feelings.

8) **B** — Lucia is using language chunking and song lyrics to build vocabulary. These are features of early production.

9) **A** — In code-switching, students mix in words from their first language when they speak their second language.

10) **D** — Common Shakespearean words like *thine, thou,* and so on may be new to ELLs and should be concretely defined before the students read the play.

11) **D** — Specially designed instruction is provided as part of an IEP but not under a 504 plan.

12) **C** — Specific comprehension deficits commonly co-occur in students with ASD.

13) **C** — Access to an audio recording of the book will help the student feel less overwhelmed and also scaffold comprehension since the focus is on listening skills rather than reading skills.

ELA Practice Test 1

1) A seventh-grade teacher asks a reading specialist how to help English language learner (ELL) students navigate the writing process, particularly the revising and editing phases. Which of the following strategies should the reading specialist recommend?

   A. encourage ELL students to read their work aloud to check for grammatical errors
   B. pair ELL students with peers whose first language is English during writing conferences
   C. allow ELL students to type their essays and use the spell-check feature
   D. provide heavy scaffolding that includes the teacher directly identifying errors for the student

2) The main goal of providing students with an arsenal of word-attack strategies is to

   A. increase oral fluency and prosody.
   B. develop automaticity through sight word awareness.
   C. improve decoding of unfamiliar words.
   D. decrease reliance on context clues.

3)

An ELA teacher is helping an interdepartmental team plan a cross-curricular lesson for a tenth-grade world history course and a tenth-grade English II course. One of the objectives is based on the following Literacy in History/Social Studies standard:

Compare the point of view of two or more authors in how they treat the same or similar topics, including which details they include and emphasize in their respective accounts (CCSS.ELA-Literacy. RH 9-10.6).

Which activity is MOST appropriate?

A. Students watch two recorded lectures by famous historians that offer two different perspectives on the fall of the Roman Empire.

B. Students read Shakespeare's *Julius Caesar* and then compare it to the information about Caesar in their history text.

C. Students read Shakespeare's *Richard III* and compare and contrast it with *Julius Caesar*.

D. Students watch a film about some aspect of Roman history and compare it with the information in their history text.

4)

An ELA teacher is trying to create learning environments that respect cultural and linguistic diversity but still aim to meet challenging state standards for oral communication. Which of the following strategies should the teacher include in her lesson planning?

A. strategies to eliminate an accent based on careful and scripted training

B. strategies to promote code-switching once students enter the school

C. opportunities to teach strategies for adjusting register based on audience

D. opportunities to recognize and correct the use of slang and idioms in speech

5)

Which of the following assessment methods would be MOST effective to gauge student writing progress over time?

A. norm-referenced assessment

B. criterion-referenced assessment

C. dynamic assessment

D. portfolio assessment

6)

Which of the following is the LEAST credible print source?

A. *Journal of the American Medical Association*

B. a PETA brochure

C. *Across Five Aprils* by Irene Hunt

D. *MLA Style Manual and Guide to Scholarly Publishing*

7)

Essays written by Jonathan Swift, John Locke, and Jean Jacques Rousseau express the ideas of

- A. the Enlightenment.
- B. the Renaissance period.
- C. the Victorian period.
- D. the Romantic period.

8)

Which of the following sentences contains a comma usage error?

- A. On her way home she stopped to pick up groceries, pay her electric bill, and buy some flowers.
- B. I used to drink coffee every morning but my office took away the coffee machine.
- C. Elizabeth will order the cake for the party after she orders the hats.
- D. My cousin, who lives in Indiana, is coming to visit this weekend.

Questions 9 – 10 refer to the following excerpt from "The Whistle" by Benjamin Franklin:

> When I was a child of seven years old, my friends on a holiday filled my pocket with coppers. I went directly to a shop where they sold toys for children; and, being charmed with the sound of a *whistle* that I met by the way in the hands of another boy, I voluntarily offered and gave all my money for one. I then came home, and went whistling all over the house, much pleased with my whistle, but disturbing all the family. My brothers and sisters and cousins, understanding the bargain I had made, told me I had given four times as much for it as it was worth; put me in mind what good things I might have bought with the rest of the money, and laughed at me so much for my folly, that I cried with vexation; and the reflection gave me more chagrin than the whistle gave me pleasure.
>
> ...
>
> When I see a beautiful, sweet-tempered girl married to an ill-natured brute of a husband, *What a pity,* say I, *that she should pay so much for a whistle!*
>
> In short, I conceive that great part of the miseries of mankind are brought upon them by the false estimates they have made of the value of things, and by their giving too much for their whistles.

Go on

9)

Which of the following does the author use to engage the reader's attention?

A. sarcasm
B. an implicit assertion
C. an anecdote
D. understatement

10)

What can be inferred about the motives of the narrator's family?

A. The family wants to teach the narrator caution in spending his money.
B. The family is simply teasing the narrator, who seems to take things too seriously.
C. The family wants to discourage the narrator from playing the whistle.
D. The family wants to make sure the narrator will not grow up to be easily influenced by others.

11)

Which type of phrase is underlined in the following sentence?

Mark, a native of Massachusetts, worked one summer at the Boston Globe.

A. appositive
B. absolute
C. prepositional
D. gerund

12)

A memoir written by a person about his/her life or about verifiable events he/she experienced, expressed in an artistic way, is an example of

A. poetry.
B. creative nonfiction.
C. fiction.
D. naturalistic fiction.

13)

Which of the following represents common knowledge that would NOT need documentation in a research paper?

A. the fact that the US Civil War lasted from 1861 to 1865
B. metadata from a study on the effects of sleep deprivation on driving
C. the results of a survey on a major university campus regarding the subject of free speech
D. a police report summarizing the murder rates from the top ten most populous cities in the United States

Questions 14 – 15 refer to the following poem, "The Scholar's Wife," by John Dryden:

> TO a deep scholar said his wife:
> "Would that I were a book, my life!
> On me then, you would sometimes look.
> But I should wish to be the book
> That you would mostly wish to see.
> Then say, what volume should I be?"
> "An Almanack," said he, "my dear;
> You know we change them every year."

14)

What is the tone of this poem?

A. irreverent

B. mean-spirited

C. scornful

D. satirical

15)

The lines "An Almanack," said he, "my dear;/You know we change them every year" are an example of a(n)

A. heroic couplet.

B. pun.

C. truism.

D. annotation.

16)

To find the comparative and superlative forms of a word, which of the following sources should a writer consult?

A. a table of contents

B. a dictionary

C. a thesaurus

D. a glossary

17)

An educator is preparing materials to give to high school students before a summer study-abroad trip. Which is the BEST topic on nonverbal communication to include?

A. an explanation of how nonverbal and verbal communication work together

B. definitions of important terms like *paralinguistics*

C. research that explains the importance of nonverbal communication

D. a list of nonverbal communication that might be different abroad from what students are used to at home

18)

Which is the BEST way to revise the underlined portion of the sentence?

Being invented in France in the early nineteenth century, the stethoscope underwent a number of reiterations before the modern form of the instrument was introduced in the 1850s.

- A. Being invented in France in the early nineteenth century,
- B. It was invented in France in the early nineteenth century,
- C. Though it was invented in France in the nineteenth century,
- D. Invented in France in the early nineteenth century,

19)

Which of the following is an example of an authentic assessment?

- A. After a unit on letter-writing, students are asked to write and send a letter to a person they know.
- B. After a unit on letter-writing, students are given an oral exam on key terms they have learned.
- C. After a unit on making inferences, students take a written multiple-choice test.
- D. After a unit on making inferences, students write an essay about what they have learned.

20)

What is one main assertion of reader-response theory?

- A. There is one correct interpretation of a literary text.
- B. Readers do not interpret literary text; they simply experience it.
- C. There is a simple process for understanding text that involves paying careful attention to the repeated elements of the text and the emotions elicited by those elements.
- D. Readers participate in the creative process; the meaning of a literary text is found partially in the author's design and partially in the reader's experience of the text.

21)

A high school English teacher assigns students a monologue to recite. What type of writing should students consult to find such a piece?

- A. a poem
- B. a novel
- C. a play
- D. an essay

Questions 22 – 23 refer to the poem "Smoke" by Henry David Thoreau:

> Light-winged Smoke, Icarian bird,
> Melting thy pinions in thy upward flight,
> Lark without song, and messenger of dawn
> Circling above the hamlets as they nest;
> Or else, departing dream, and shadowy form
> Of midnight vision, gathering up thy skirts;
> By night star-veiling, and by day
> Darkening the light and blotting out the sun;
> Go thou my incense upward from this hearth,
> And ask the gods to pardon this clear flame.

22)

Which of the following BEST describes this poem?

- A. a sonnet
- B. an extended metaphor
- C. a ballad
- D. an ironic statement

23)

The word *pinions* means

- A. restraints that tie the arms to the body.
- B. cuts to the end of a bird's wing that prevent it from flying.
- C. the fall of Icarus.
- D. the outer feathers on a bird's wing.

24)

While helping a seventh-grade student revise his essay, a reading specialist notices that he uses slang and regional dialect throughout. Which of the following is the BEST course of action for the reading specialist to take?

- A. Review the fundamentals of proper English and have him rewrite the essay.
- B. Encourage him to think about the fundamental differences between speaking and writing.
- C. Ask him to consider his audience and revise the essay using more formal language.
- D. Provide time to give him more explicit instruction in grammar and mechanics.

Questions 25 – 27 refer to the first stanza of the poem "The Second Coming" by William Butler Yeats:

> Turning and turning in the widening gyre
> The falcon cannot hear the falconer;
> Things fall apart; the centre cannot hold;
> Mere anarchy is loosed upon the world,
> The blood-dimmed tide is loosed, and everywhere
> The ceremony of innocence is drowned;
> The best lack all conviction, while the worst
> Are full of passionate intensity.

25)

"The blood-dimmed tide is loosed" is

- A. a metaphor.
- B. hyperbole.
- C. an understatement.
- D. a simile.

26)

"The Second Coming" is written in

- A. rhyming couplets.
- B. blank verse.
- C. quatrains.
- D. free verse.

27)

The novel *Things Fall Apart* by Chinua Achebe takes its title from this poem. What is the connection between the poem and the novel?

- A. The novel *Things Fall Apart* relates the decline of the British monarchy.
- B. In the novel *Things Fall Apart*, the account of disease and suffering in Africa has the same emotional effect as Yeats' poem.
- C. The novel *Things Fall Apart* shows the destructive impact of British imperialism on the culture of people in Africa.
- D. The Atlantic slave trade, which caused the destruction of many African villages, is described in the novel *Things Fall Apart*; Achebe used Yeats' poem to draw parallels to the suffering of its victims.

28)

An ELA teacher is co-planning with a special education teacher to meet the needs of a student with dysgraphia. Which of the following scaffolds is MOST appropriate to include in the plan?

A. a text reader
B. large-print text
C. speech-to-text software
D. texts at a lower Lexile level

29)

Which introduction to a quotation within the body of a research paper would sound the MOST academic and lend credibility to the source?

A. In their online article for the medical supply company, Dr. Smith and Dr. Jones indicate that . . .
B. Several well-known authors agree with the following assertion:
C. Medical professionals all across the United States have testified that . . .
D. Dr. Frank Johnson, orthopedic surgeon from Medical University, asserts in his latest article that the . . .

30)

James Russell Lowell is MOST closely associated with which group of poets?

A. the transcendentalist poets
B. the Fireside poets
C. the Imagists
D. the Beat poets

31)

Which sentence does NOT contain an error?

A. My sister and my best friend lives in Chicago.
B. My parents or my brother is going to pick me up from the airport.
C. Neither of the students refuse to take the exam.
D. The team were playing a great game until the rain started.

32)

Which of the following would make the greatest impact on students' writing abilities?

A. inviting professional writers to share their experiences with the class
B. setting aside time each day for sentence diagramming and oral drills
C. having students write only about topics they care about deeply
D. allowing time for writing each day or during each class

33)

John Dryden and John Milton are British writers of the

A. Romantic period.

B. Restoration period.

C. Elizabethan age.

D. Victorian era.

Questions 34 – 36 refer to the initial lines from the poem "The Pyramids of Egypt," in *Introductory to Egypt, Nubia, and Abyssinia* by Philip Freneau:

> 'TIS darkness all, with hateful silence joined—
> Here drowsy bats enjoy a dull repose,
> And marble coffins, vacant of their bones,
> Show where the royal dead in ruin lay!

34)

Which statement BEST summarizes how imagery conveys the author's idea of the Egyptian pyramids?

A. The image of royal people who are dead is frightening and disturbing.

B. The imagery of coffins reveals the pointlessness of having power.

C. The imagery of tombs suggests emptiness and ruin.

D. The image of hateful silence suggests sadness and danger.

35)

How would a semantic map of the poem help students understand the poet's use of concrete imagery to suggest an abstract idea?

A. With "hateful silence" in the center circle, students could fill in the other circles with the concrete details related to hateful silence.

B. Students could fill in the circles with the images of the poem.

C. Students could pull out all of the adjectives and nouns in the poem; then draw lines that link the adjectives to the nouns they modify.

D. Students could fill the circles with each word that is related to Egyptian pyramids.

36)

If a teacher asks her students to use details of this poem to explain how the words *darkness*, *coffins*, and *silence* make them feel, which critical approach is she using?

A. formalism

B. reader-response

C. semiotic analysis

D. Marxist criticism

37)

A reading specialist providing feedback to an eighth-grade teacher suggests that students should read aloud pieces they have written. The reading specialist is MOST likely suggesting this because

A. students of this age are still developing oral language skills.

B. the teacher should grade writing only after hearing it read aloud.

C. this is a simple way for students to publish their work.

D. oral reading is the optimal time for mechanics instruction.

38)

Which of the following topics is appropriate for a four- to six-page research paper?

A. American poetry

B. the causes of WWI

C. the dangers of fad diets

D. the development of grammar from the 1900s forward

Questions 39 – 40 refer to the introductory sentences below from Louisa May Alcott's "Street Scenes in Washington":

> THE MULES were my especial delight; and an hour's study of a constant succession of them introduced me to many of their characteristics; for six of these odd little beasts drew each army wagon and went hopping like frogs through the stream of mud that gently rolled along the street. The coquettish mule had small feet, a nicely trimmed tassel of a tail, perked-up ears, and seemed much given to little tosses of the head, affected skips and prances; and, if he wore the bells or were bedizened with a bit of finery, put on as many airs as any belle. The moral mule was a stout, hard-working creature, always tugging with all his might, often pulling away after the rest had stopped, laboring under the conscientious delusion that food for the entire army depended upon his private exertions. I respected this style of mule; and, had I possessed a juicy cabbage, would have pressed it upon him with thanks for his excellent example.

39)

What is Louisa May Alcott's purpose in this section of text from "Street Scenes in Washington"?

A. to inform readers about the activity on the streets of Washington

B. to persuade readers that life in the city is fascinating

C. to convince people to take the time to observe human activity

D. to express her thoughts as she observes mules on a street in Washington

40)

How does Louisa May Alcott organize the details in this section of text?

A. according to the chronology of events

B. from the general (a wagon pulled by mules, moving along the street) to the specific (each specific mule)

C. from the most important—the most attractive mule—to the least important mule

D. spatially, from the left side of the street to the right side

41)

Which is the BEST way to revise the underlined portion of the sentence?

During the Civil War, a significant number of soldiers died during battle; indeed, large numbers of soldiers and civilians fell ill and died as a result of living conditions during the war.

A. in addition,

B. therefore,

C. however,

D. on the other hand,

42)

A ninth-grade English teacher asks students to submit possible topics for their 2,000-word research papers. One student submits the topic of "television." What is the BEST feedback for the teacher to provide?

A. think about how to narrow the focus

B. develop a pro-con list based on the topic

C. focus on gathering primary sources

D. begin with an outline to guide drafting

43)

A teacher wants to encourage a performer in a high school production to recognize a character tag per the script. Which question could the teacher ask with this aim in mind?

A. What phrase does your character repeat throughout the play?

B. What motivation does your character have for behaving this way?

C. What do the other characters in the play think about your character?

D. What interactions does your character have with the setting?

44)

In a connected text, a middle school student receiving supplemental reading instruction encounters the word *admiration*. Which strategy should the interventionist encourage the student to use to determine the meaning of this unknown word?

A. syllabication
B. identifying roots and affixes
C. sematic cueing
D. emphasizing onset and rime

45)

One characteristic of metaphysical poetry is

A. using a serious, stern tone.
B. addressing the practical, everyday concerns of life.
C. addressing the value of scientific discoveries.
D. using paradoxes and puns as well as everyday language.

46)

Which activity BEST aligns with the goal of building confidence in students who are nervous about speaking in front of a group?

A. whole-class discussion
B. small-group presentation
C. reader's theater
D. Socratic seminar

47)

While observing writing conferences in a high school classroom, a teacher hears a student suggest to a peer that he delete an irrelevant sentence from his essay. The teacher would MOST likely praise the student for her suggestion to improve the essay's

A. tone.
B. organization.
C. style.
D. focus.

48)

Consider the first lines (below) of "Autumn" from *The Belfry of Bruges and Other Poems* by Henry Wadsworth Longfellow. What sound device is used in the line "With banners, by great gales incessant fanned"?

> THOU comest, Autumn, heralded by the rain,
> With banners, by great gales incessant fanned,
> Brighter than brightest silks of Samarcand,
> And stately oxen harnessed to thy wain!

- A. assonance
- B. mood
- C. symbolism
- D. tone

49)

Which citation shows the correct way to cite a direct quote in APA style?

- A. (Harper)
- B. (Harper, p. 22)
- C. (Harper, 2006, p. 22)
- D. (Harper, page 22)

50)

A sixth-grade student receiving literacy interventions writes the following introductory paragraph for his autobiographical essay:

My name is Joel my friends sometimes call me Joe. I have lived in Boston all my life I enjoy baseball fishing and marshal arts. After school. I live in a large house my two brothers live there to.

Which type of targeted mechanics instruction should the interventionist plan?

- A. basic orthography
- B. sentence structure
- C. basic capitalization
- D. preposition use

51)

Which assessment would be MOST valid in measuring foundational reading skills?

- A. OLSAT
- B. DIBELS
- C. WrAP
- D. COGAT

Questions 52 – 53 refer to the following stanzas from "The Haunted Oak" by Paul Laurence Dunbar:

> PRAY why are you so bare, so bare,
> Oh bough of the old oak-tree;
> And why, when I go through the shade you throw,
> Runs a shudder over me?
>
> My leaves were green as the best, I trow,
> And sap ran free in my veins,
> But I saw in the moonlight dim and weird
> A guiltless victim's pains.
>
> I bent me down to hear his sigh;
> I shook with his gurgling moan,
> And I trembled sore when they rode away,
> And left him here alone.
>
> ...
>
> I feel the rope against my bark,
> And the weight of him in my grain,
> I feel the throe of his final woe
> The touch of my own last pain.
>
> And never more shall leaves come forth
> On a bough that bears the ban;
> I am burned with dread, I am dried and dead,
> From the curse of a guiltless man.

52)

The initial speaker of the poem asks an old oak tree "why are you so bare, so bare ... ?" When a student explains she is convinced that the old oak tree is bare because an innocent man was hung on one of the tree's branches, she is

- A. making an inference.
- B. making a prediction.
- C. stating a theme of the poem.
- D. stating a pattern in the poem.

53)

The student elaborates on her explanation by quoting the lines, "I feel the rope against my bark,/And the weight of him in my grain[.]" In doing so, she is

- A. analyzing the point of view.
- B. demonstrating the perspective of the author.
- C. showing the rhyme scheme.
- D. supporting her explanation with textual evidence.

54) A ninth-grade ELA teacher wants to help the class, which has limited experience with public speaking, prepare for a short speaking assignment. Which strategy is MOST likely to be helpful to students?

A. write the speech down and then recite it from memory
B. write the speech down and read it verbatim
C. write key points of the speech on note cards to refer to as necessary
D. write questions you anticipate from the audience to refer to as necessary

55) Which of the following strategies is MOST appropriate for helping students acquire and retain content-specific vocabulary words?

A. providing students with a thesaurus to refer to as they encounter new vocabulary
B. teaching students some of the most commonly used roots and affixes for content-area words
C. encouraging students to read fiction texts on similar topics that feature content-area words
D. giving students a brief refresher on the basics of the graphophonic cueing system

56) What is the BEST reason to include reference to counterclaims in argumentative writing?

A. to show mastery of the subject matter
B. to promote the use of ethos appeals
C. to praise alternate perspectives
D. to offer reasonable refutations

57) Which of the following parts of speech describes how *travels* is used in the following sentence?

Abby's travels in Asia provided her the opportunity to try many foods that she would not have been able to try at home in the United States.

A. verb
B. noun
C. adjective
D. adverb

58)

In which type of writing would students be MOST likely to use a dialect or register and still communicate a message effectively?

A. an expository essay

B. a free-verse poem

C. a research paper

D. a biographical essay

59)

Which strategy would be MOST helpful for a student who has just arrived in the US who is in the earliest stage of second-language acquisition?

A. participating in peer tutoring

B. receiving extra time for test completion

C. completing a graphic organizer

D. using a picture dictionary

Question 60 is based on the following excerpt from the short story "The Legend of Sleepy Hollow" by Washington Irving:

> I recollect that, when a stripling, my first exploit in squirrel-shooting was in a grove of tall walnut-trees that shades one side of the valley. I had wandered into it at noontime, when all nature is peculiarly quiet, and was startled by the roar of my own gun, as it broke the Sabbath stillness around and was prolonged and reverberated by the angry echoes. If ever I should wish for a retreat whither I might steal from the world and its distractions, and dream quietly away the remnant of a troubled life, I know of none more promising than this little valley.

60)

Which of the following BEST describes the organization of the passage?

A. It is a description that includes sensory detail.

B. The text is the sequence of events during a day of squirrel shooting.

C. The text is organized as an explanation of the reasons people seek solitude.

D. The echoing roar of the gun is contrasted to the stillness of the little valley.

61)

Which activity BEST meets the goals of students using content-area vocabulary in an authentic context?

A. writing a letter to a pen pal in another nation

B. creating a website to teach others about parts of a cell

C. drafting an essay about Spanish colonies in the Americas

D. making a model of a proposed community irrigation plan

62)

An example of satirical prose is

A. *The Last of the Mohicans.*

B. *Their Eyes Were Watching God.*

C. *The Rime of the Ancient Mariner.*

D. *Gulliver's Travels.*

63)

A reading specialist is working with a high school English teacher to develop more rigorous assessment items. The goal is to write questions that fall within Benjamin Bloom's second level of understanding. Which of the following assessment items meets this cognitive-level goal?

A. What is the name for writing that tries to persuade others?

B. Critique the following persuasive essay for its use of rhetorical conventions.

C. Write a three-sentence summary of the persuasive essay.

D. Create an outline for a persuasive essay.

64)

A high school teacher requires students to have research paper topics approved beforehand. In designing a form for students to fill out about their proposed topics, which is the BEST question to include?

A. What sources are available regarding this topic?

B. How did you become interested in this topic?

C. What do you already know about this topic?

D. Who else would be interested in this topic?

65)

Which type of clause is underlined in the following sentence?

Alice missed the most exciting part of the game; <u>consequently, she returned to the car disappointed</u>.

A. noun clause

B. adverb clause

C. adjective clause

D. independent clause

66)

A ninth-grade student gives an oral presentation to her English class full of slang that mocks the subject matter. Under which rubric category would the teacher MOST likely leave feedback for improvement?

A. tone
B. clarity
C. conciseness
D. articulation

Questions 67 – 68 refer to the following sections from the essay "On Lying News-Writers," from *The Idler* by Samuel Johnson:

> NO species of literary men has lately been so much multiplied as the writers of news. Not many years ago the nation was content with one gazette; but now we have not only in the metropolis papers for every morning and every evening, but almost every large town has its weekly historian, who regularly circulates his periodical intelligence, and fills the villages of his district with conjectures on the events of war, and with debates on the true interest of Europe.
>
> To write news in its perfection requires such a combination of qualities, that a man completely fitted for the task is not always to be found. In Sir Henry Wotton's jocular definition, "An ambassador is said to be a man of virtue sent abroad to tell lies for the advantage of his country; a news writer is a man without virtue, who writes lies at home for his own profit." To these compositions is required neither genius nor knowledge, neither industry nor sprightliness; but contempt of shame and indifference to truth are absolutely necessary. He who by a long familiarity with infamy has obtained these qualities, may confidently tell to-day what he intends to contradict to-morrow; he may affirm fearlessly what he knows that he shall be obliged to recant, and may write letters from Amsterdam or Dresden to himself.
>
> In a time of war the nation is always of one mind, eager to hear something good of themselves and ill of the enemy. At this time the task of news-writers is easy; they have nothing to do but to tell that a battle is expected, and afterward that a battle has been fought, in which we and our friends, whether conquering or conquered, did all, and our enemies did nothing.
>
> Among the calamities of war may be justly numbered the diminution of the love of truth, by the falsehoods which interest dictates and credulity encourages. A peace will equally leave the warrior and relater of wars destitute of employment; and I know not whether more is to be dreaded from the streets filled with soldiers accustomed to plunder, or from garrets filled with scribblers accustomed to lie.

67)

The author's view of news writers is

A. stated explicitly.
B. implicit.
C. revealed by the point of view.
D. indicated by the matter-of-fact tone.

68)

What kind of appeal does Johnson use to support his perspective?

A. ethical appeal
B. logical appeal
C. emotional appeal
D. evidential appeal

69)

Which type of sentence is the following?

The carpet's coloring was rich, and its pattern was complex.

A. simple
B. complex
C. compound
D. compound-complex

70)

During which period of British literature were many epic poems about heroes and morality shared orally?

A. Anglo-Saxon
B. Victorian
C. Romantic
D. Renaissance

71)

Which of the words from the following sentence is slang?

It's a drag to do homework on the weekend, but I won't pass the class if I spend all day watching TV.

A. drag
B. homework
C. weekend
D. pass

72)

Which early literacy activity would be conducted FIRST in terms of developmental sequence?

- A. students reading high-frequency sight words from a chart
- B. students reciting the sound of each letter in sequence
- C. students manipulating words through phoneme substitution
- D. students clapping out onset and rime as a word is spoken

Questions 73 – 74 refer to the following excerpt from *Anecdotes of the Late Samuel Johnson* by Hester Thrale.

> There is no private house in which people can enjoy themselves so well as at a capital tavern. Let there be ever so great plenty of good things, ever so much grandeur, ever so much elegance, ever so much desire that everybody should be easy, in the nature of things it cannot be: there must always be some degree of care and anxiety. The master of the house is anxious to entertain his guests—the guests are anxious to be agreeable to him; and no man, but a very impudent dog indeed, can as freely command what is in another man's house as if it was his own. Whereas, at a tavern, there is a general freedom from anxiety. You are sure you are welcome; and the more noise you make, the more trouble you give, the more good things you call for, the welcomer you are. No servants will attend you with the alacrity which waiters do, who are incited by the prospect of an immediate reward in proportion as they please. No, sir, there is nothing which has yet been contrived by man, by which so much happiness is produced as by a good tavern or inn.

73)

What is the author implying about taverns in this passage?

- A. People enjoy themselves in taverns because they are relaxed and not worried about pleasing anyone.
- B. People want to behave rudely, like impudent dogs, at house parties but do not because they will be thrown out.
- C. People who give house parties make their guests uncomfortable by hovering over them.
- D. People are only happy in taverns because they can boss around the waiters, who will listen because they want tips.

74)

Which organizational pattern is Johnson using in this section of text?

- A. sequential
- B. compare and contrast
- C. cause and effect
- D. chronological

75)

While giving oral presentations, students should be encouraged to look at the

- A. visual aid they are showing.
- B. audience in front of them.
- C. farthest wall in the room.
- D. person sitting closest to them.

76)

The main goal of a K-W-L chart is to help students

- A. organize new vocabulary based on similar semantic and syntactic qualities.
- B. use a set framework for activating background knowledge, setting a purpose, and summarizing.
- C. refer to a set list of fix-up strategies and then choose the most appropriate one for the situation.
- D. learn how to make inferences, identify purpose, and distinguish between fact and opinion.

77)

Harun is writing an essay about the migration patterns of birds. Which of the following facts would NOT be relevant to his research?

- A. Within a species, the tendency to migrate might vary by the location of each population, as populations in areas that are warm year-round may not need to migrate in pursuit of food.
- B. Of the species of bird that migrate, not all do so by flying: some bird species, such as the penguin, migrate in other ways, like by swimming.
- C. Prior to the late eighteenth century, many people believed that birds hibernated during the winter; only later did they accept migration as an explanation for the absence of birds during winter.
- D. Migration patterns may vary within a bird species based on age and gender.

78)

A standardized assessment instrument that measures reading and language skills is widely used across the nation. Recently, educators have become critical of the assessment results and their ability to screen for possible reading disabilities, noting that many students are being falsely identified. What additional information would be MOST helpful for the educators to gather regarding the norm-referenced assessment to determine its current efficacy?

- A. when the test was last calibrated with a representative norming group
- B. which other schools and districts are using the assessment
- C. how many questions the assessment has at each cognitive level
- D. which other norm-referenced assessments are similar to the test

79)

Which type of sentence is the following?

Although the politician denied that he intended to run for the presidency, he behaved as if he might.

A. simple
B. complex
C. compound
D. compound-complex

80)

In the following sentence, the prefix *pre–* indicates that the evaluation will take place at which time?

The patient's preoperative evaluation is scheduled for next Wednesday.

A. before the operation
B. after the operation
C. during the operation
D. at the end of the operation

Questions 81 – 82 refer to the speech "The Man with the Muck-rake" by Theodore Roosevelt, delivered April 14, 1906:

> Over a century ago Washington laid the corner stone of the Capitol in what was then little more than a tract of wooded wilderness here beside the Potomac. We now find it necessary to provide by great additional buildings for the business of the government.
>
> This growth in the need for the housing of the government is but a proof and example of the way in which the nation has grown and the sphere of action of the national government has grown. We now administer the affairs of a nation in which the extraordinary growth of population has been outstripped by the growth of wealth in complex interests. The material problems that face us today are not such as they were in Washington's time, but the underlying facts of human nature are the same now as they were then. Under altered external form we war with the same tendencies toward evil that were evident in Washington's time, and are helped by the same tendencies for good. It is about some of these that I wish to say a word today.

81)

What is the central idea of Roosevelt's speech?

A. The growth of the United States has resulted in a war between the conflicting interests of many groups in government.

B. While the US government and population have grown, the United States continues to deal with the basic characteristics of human nature, both positive and negative.

C. Many Americans have gained great wealth and are now attempting to control the government.

D. The country has grown so fast and has acquired so much wealth that the government is struggling to deal with rising inequality between the wealthy and the poor.

82)

Roosevelt mentions construction of "great additional buildings for the business of government" to emphasize

A. changes that have taken place in the type of government.

B. the complexity of democratic principles.

C. the power of the United States as a world leader.

D. the growth of the United States.

83)

The following statement reflects the usage of which logical fallacy?

The corruption of the leadership is inevitable because a fish rots from the head down.

A. hasty generalization

B. false analogy

C. irrelevant argument (*non-sequitur*)

D. false cause (*post hoc, ergo propter hoc*)

84)

The underlined phrase in the sentence below functions as which of the following parts of speech?

<u>To save lots of money</u>, *the young family shopped for clothing at the local thrift store.*

A. noun

B. pronoun

C. adjective

D. adverb

85)

Which skill is BEST assessed via running records?

A. comprehension
B. mechanics
C. oral fluency
D. sentence structure

86)

Tenth-graders have been assigned a presentation that gives biographical information about Shakespeare. Which type of visual aid is likely to be MOST effective for this purpose?

A. a map showing the different places Shakespeare lived throughout his life
B. a thought cloud that shows words that come to mind when people think of Shakespeare
C. a timeline that shows significant events in Shakespeare's life
D. a Venn diagram comparing Shakespeare's major works

87)

Which author is MOST closely associated with the regional "local color" movement of the late nineteenth century in the United States?

A. Edith Wharton
B. T.S. Eliot
C. Willa Cather
D. Cormac McCarthy

88)

An ELA teacher is working with a small group of students and asks them to use each of the bold headings in their textbook to generate questions they will answer after reading the chapter. This is a strategy to help students do what?

A. read with purpose
B. activate background knowledge
C. apply fix-up strategies
D. use context clues

89)

An eighth-grade teacher is preparing for a writing conference and notices that a student's essay contains several sentences unrelated to the thesis. What would MOST likely be the focus of the writing conference?

A. support
B. mechanics
C. organization
D. unity

90)

Which of the following scaffolding techniques is LEAST effective in presenting new content to students learning English?

A. using modified reading materials

B. previewing vocabulary prior to a lesson

C. providing students with an outline for notes

D. performing regular checks for understanding

91)

At the start of each school year, all students are given a reading assessment to identify those at possible risk for reading difficulties. What is this process called?

A. universal screening

B. multi-tiered system of supports

C. response to intervention

D. diagnostic testing

Questions 92 – 93 refer to the speech "On Women's Right to Vote" by Susan B. Anthony, 1873:

> Friends and fellow citizens: I stand before you tonight under indictment for the alleged crime of having voted at the last presidential election, without having a lawful right to vote. It shall be my work this evening to prove to you that in thus voting, I not only committed no crime, but, instead, simply exercised my citizen's rights, guaranteed to me and all United States citizens by the National Constitution, beyond the power of any state to deny.
>
> The only question left to be settled now is: Are women persons? And I hardly believe any of our opponents will have the hardihood to say they are not. Being persons, then, women are citizens; and no state has a right to make any law, or to enforce any old law, that shall abridge their privileges or immunities. Hence, every discrimination against women in the constitutions and laws of the several states is today null and void, precisely as is every one against Negroes.

92)

What is the purpose of Susan B. Anthony's speech?

A. to express her anger about being arrested

B. to inform people about the injustice women face

C. to persuade women to continue to fight against all discrimination

D. to convince others that she has the lawful right to vote

93)

Which TWO rhetorical strategies does Susan B. Anthony use? Select ALL that apply.

A. rhetorical question
B. understatement
C. parallelism
D. amplification

94)

In a persuasive text, when one of the main arguments is based on the premise that if one thing happens, a series of other things will automatically happen, the reasoning may be referred to as

A. a hasty generalization.
B. dichotomous thinking.
C. a slippery slope.
D. an emotional appeal.

95)

Which of the following is a standardized assessment instrument?

A. a curriculum-based assessment
B. a teacher-created summative assessment
C. the Iowa Test of Basic Skills
D. an exit ticket given at the end of a lesson

96)

A high school educator teaching a dual-credit US history course notices students are struggling to understand the college-level textbook. Which of the following strategies would be MOST appropriate to help the students?

A. focusing the class's attention on multimedia texts instead of written information
B. giving students explicit strategies, such as the SQ3R method
C. reading most of the textbook aloud in class
D. switching to another textbook for the rest of the year

97)

Inflection in speaking refers to changes in

A. nonverbal cues.
B. tone or pitch.
C. dialect or vernacular.
D. syntax.

98)

Which of the following sentences indicates the end of a sequence?

A. Our ultimate objective was to find a quality coat at an affordable price.

B. We chose this particular restaurant because of its outdoor seating.

C. Finally, we were able to settle in to enjoy the movie.

D. Initially, it seemed unlikely that we'd be able to keep the puppy.

99)

A tenth-grade English teacher is beginning a unit where students will be reading a novel that includes challenging content-specific vocabulary. What is the BEST strategy for the teacher to employ?

A. instruct students in a text annotation system to help them link unknown words and context clues

B. rely on incidental vocabulary learning as students read the text independently at their own pace

C. preteach the most frequently used words prior to asking students to begin reading the text

D. give frequent vocabulary quizzes covering important terms as students read the novel

Question 100 refers to the following text:

Communicating with any human being in crisis—whether that crisis is physical or emotional—is going to be more difficult than normal, everyday communication. Thus, emergency responders and medical practitioners, like many other social service providers, need to learn how to be sensitive in interpersonal communication. Here are some tips about how to hone your craft as a communicator while working with people in crisis. These tips can also be used for everyday communication.

First, it is essential that you are aware of cultural differences. In some cultures, direct eye contact can be unsettling or disrespectful. People from different cultures may have different comfort levels with personal space: some might find physical closeness comforting; others might find it threatening. Your body language speaks volumes. Be sure you are aware of the symbolic nature of your posture, hand motions, and gestures.

It is also important to enunciate your verbal statements and directions in a clear, relevant way. Use terminology and directions that a patient will understand, and avoid lofty medical jargon. Believe it or not, you also want to be honest with the person in crisis, even if the conditions are dire. Also explain, if possible, what you might do to help alleviate even the most drastic conditions so that the person feels supported. Lastly, and most importantly, be prepared to listen. Even if there is a language barrier, condition, or disability limiting your communication with the person in crisis, try to position yourself as an active listener. These tips will help you support people who need clarity and sensitivity.

100)

What is the BEST summary of the passage?

A. In some cultures, direct eye contact can be unsettling or disrespectful.

B. Posture, hand motions, and gestures can symbolize respect or disrespect.

C. Medical practitioners must learn to be sensitive with people who are in crisis.

D. Medical practitioners should give clear directions and avoid using lofty medical jargon.

Answer Key

1)
B Having English language learners (ELLs) review their work with a peer whose first language is English is an effective way to use homogenous grouping and actively involve ELLs in the revision process.

2)
C The main purpose of helping students develop a variety of word-attack strategies is to improve decoding of unfamiliar words.

3)
B Studying Shakespeare's *Julius Caesar* and comparing it to the relevant information in the history text involves two different texts by two different authors. Student can compare things, such as purpose (inform versus entertain), and why certain points are or are not emphasized.

4)
C Students should understand that oral communication in different dialects and registers is not right or wrong, good or bad. Students should adjust their communication style based on audience and situation.

5)
D A portfolio shows student progress over a span of time. Writing samples will hopefully show growth and increased proficiency and complexity.

6)
B A brochure from PETA, a well-known advocacy group for animals, is not a credible print source because it is potentially biased.

7)
A The writers Jonathan Swift, John Locke, and Jean Jacques Rousseau expressed the belief that social problems can be solved by the use of reason.

8)
B This compound sentence requires a comma before the conjunction *but*.

9)
C   The author tells the short story, or anecdote, of overpaying for an appealing toy, which illustrates his main point.

10)
C   The narrator played the whistle less because he was upset about spending too much for it.

11)
A   The phrase *a native of Massachusetts* renames the noun *Mark*.

12)
B   Creative nonfiction is based in truth and expressed in a compelling, artistic way.

13)
A   The dates of the US Civil War are widely known and do not need documentation.

14)
D   The husband is using humor and exaggeration to ridicule his wife for seeking attention.

15)
A   A heroic couplet is a pair of rhyming lines written in iambic pentameter.

16)
B   One of the features of the dictionary is the identification of comparatives and superlatives.

17)
D   Certain types of nonverbal communication, such as shaking hands and appropriate social space, can differ from place to place.

18)
D   *Invented*, the past participle of *invent*, appropriately introduces this participial phrase that provides more information about the subject of the sentence (*stethoscope*).

19)
A   Writing and sending a letter after a unit on letter-writing is an authentic assessment because it evaluates student knowledge in a relevant and real-world way.

20)
D   Some of the ways readers participate in the creative process are by imagining, remembering, and feeling what the text reminds them about in their own experiences. The artistic choices of the author inspire the reader's reflections.

21)
C   Drama is most likely to contain a monologue, which is a lengthy speech made by a single person.

22)
B   Thoreau is using the Icarian bird as a vehicle to describe smoke. The reader needs to ask how smoke is like a bird that circles, becomes a shadowy form at night, and darkens the morning sky.

Answer Key

23) D Pinions are the outer feathers on a bird's wing. The poem references the story of Icarus, whose wings melted when he flew too close to the sun.

24) C Considering audience will help the student think about how to best communicate his message clearly to the reader.

25) A "The blood-dimmed tide is loosed" is a metaphor to describe what happens when "[t]hings fall apart" and "innocence is drowned"; no literal tide of blood is streaming.

26) D The poem follows no regular rhyme scheme or form, making it free verse.

27) C The novel depicts the culture of the Igbo people being destroyed by the British missionaries and colonists who impose their ideas on the Igbo.

28) C Speech-to-text software would allow the student with dysgraphia to dictate written assignments that can be converted to text.

29) D This introduction, which states the doctor's name and field of medicine, provides enough information to legitimize Dr. Johnson as an authoritative source.

30) B Fireside poets, like Longfellow, Lowell, and Bryant, wrote about the nineteenth-century United States, expressed views on political issues, and used conventional forms.

31) B The verb *is* agrees with the closest subject—in this case, the singular noun *brother*.

32) D Writing as much as possible is one of the best ways to improve writing ability.

33) B The eighteenth-century Restoration period is also referred to as the Neoclassical period or the Age of Satire.

34) C The imagery of the tombs effectively summarizes and connects to this broader idea of the Egyptian pyramids.

35) A A semantic map helps students see the connections or relationships between words and concepts. By placing an abstract phrase in the center of the map, students can then build onto it by adding the concrete images that contribute to their understanding of the abstract elements of the poem.

36) B Reader-response emphasizes the responses readers have to the details of a text.

37) C Reading work aloud is one simple and immediate way for students to publish their work, which is the last stage of the writing process. Publishing also provides a link between reading and writing.

38) C The dangers of fad diets could probably be covered adequately in four to six pages. The other topics are too broad to be covered in such a short paper.

39) D The author is expressing her thoughts, saying that she is delighted by the mules and sharing what she notices.

40) B The author begins by saying that she studies the mules that are pulling a wagon (the general); then she discusses each mule (the specific).

41) A *In addition* is the appropriate introductory phrase as it signifies the additive relationship between the two clauses.

42) A "Television" is too broad a topic for a 2,000-word research paper, so the best feedback is to ask the student to think about how to narrow the focus.

43) A Character tags are repeated verbal devices that help make a character distinct and unique.

44) B The root word *admire* and the suffix *–ion* could be used to help this student derive meaning from this word.

45) D Metaphysical poetry is noted for plays on words and complex ideas about the contradictions of life.

46) B Small-group presentations will enable students to practice speaking in front of a small group before speaking in front of a larger group.

47) D This student is helping her peer ensure his writing remains true to its overall point or focus.

48) A Assonance is the repetition of the /an/ sound in the words *banners*, *incessant*, and *fanned*.

Answer Key

49) C — In APA format, the author's last name, date, and page number are needed in the in-text citation.

50) B — The student's writing is mostly run-on sentences and fragments, indicating that he needs explicit instruction in sentence structure.

51) B — The Dynamic Indicators of Basic Early Literacy Skills (DIBELS) is an oral assessment that can be used for students in grades K – 8.

52) A — The poet does not state that a person was hung on a bough of the oak tree; the reader is using her knowledge of hangings as well as details revealed in subsequent stanzas to infer this.

53) D — A quotation from the text that supports a particular interpretation is textual evidence.

54) C — Writing key points on note cards will allow students to have some support but still give an engaging speech.

55) B — Morphemes like *micro* and *macro* and many other common roots and affixes can help students as they encounter content-area words.

56) D — Refuting counterclaims is a useful rhetorical technique as it directly addresses the opposition.

57) B — *Travels* functions as a noun; it is the subject of the sentence.

58) B — Informal language could communicate a message effectively in a free-verse poem, which is written without a set structure.

59) D — A student in the earliest preproduction, or "silent period," of second language acquisition would benefit most from a picture dictionary, which will help the student understand basic directions and classroom routines.

60) D — The passage begins with the narrator entering the grove of trees. Then, when the narrator fires his gun, he says the sound "broke the Sabbath stillness around and was prolonged and reverberated by the angry echoes." The last sentence says the place would be a perfect retreat.

61) B — Creating the website would enable students to use science content-area words to describe cells, and the website is an authentic context.

62)
D *Gulliver's Travels* is a satire of British society, human nature, and adventure tales.

63)
C Summarizing falls within Bloom's second level of understanding.

64)
A This question is essential because students must be able to find adequate sources of information on a topic in order to compose a research paper.

65)
D The underlined clause is independent. Remember, a semicolon must be preceded AND followed by an independent clause.

66)
A Tone refers to the attitude presented in the speech toward the subject matter. This student's tone is largely inappropriate for the classroom context.

67)
A The author directly states, "Among the calamities of war may be justly numbered the diminution of the love of truth, by the falsehoods which interest dictates and credulity encourages. . . . I know not whether more is to be dreaded from the streets filled with soldiers accustomed to plunder, or from garrets filled with scribblers accustomed to lie."

68)
A Johnson quotes someone who was apparently a respected, credible figure in his time: "In Sir Henry Wotton's jocular definition, 'An ambassador is said to be a man of virtue sent abroad to tell lies for the advantage of his country; a news writer is a man without virtue, who writes lies at home for his own profit.'"

69)
C Two independent clauses are divided properly with the coordinating conjunction *and*.

70)
A Some of these Anglo-Saxon epics, like *Beowulf*, were eventually recorded in the written word.

71)
A In the sentence, *drag* is used as a slang term that means "an annoying or boring task."

72)
D Clapping out onset and rime is a very basic and simple activity to promote beginning phonemic awareness. Students can clap out /d/ /og/.

73)
A The text says that at house parties, "there must always be some degree of care and anxiety. . . . Whereas, at a tavern, there is a general freedom from anxiety. You are sure you are welcome. . . ."

Answer Key 213

74)

B Socializing at a tavern is contrasted with the practice of socializing at someone's house during a house party.

75)

B During oral presentations, speakers should maintain eye contact with the audience throughout the presentation.

76)

B Students use a framework to activate background knowledge ("what I already know"), set a purpose for reading ("what I want to know"), and summarize what they have learned ("what I learned").

77)

C Though it is interesting, the history of humanity's understanding of bird migration is not necessarily relevant to an essay about bird migration.

78)

A The norms established by the test makers may not be current if the test was last calibrated a long time ago.

79)

B This sentence has one independent clause and three dependent clauses, so it is a complex sentence.

80)

A The prefix *pre-* means "before."

81)

B Roosevelt states his purpose when he says, "we war with the same tendencies toward evil that were evident in Washington's time, and are helped by the same tendencies for good. It is about some of these that I wish to say a word today."

82)

D According to the text, additional government buildings have been necessary to accommodate the growth in government activity that has accompanied the corresponding growth of the country.

83)

B A rotting fish is not analogous to a position of leadership.

84)

D The phrase *to save lots of money* is modifying the verb *shopped* and explains why the young family shopped at the local thrift store. (Note that all introductory infinitive phrases are adverbial.)

85)

C Running records are oral reading checks that assess rate, accuracy, and prosody.

86)

C A timeline of Shakespeare's life is likely the most effective visual aid since the presentation is biographical in nature and would give the most information about the author's life as a whole.

87)

C Cather is known for her novels that focus on life on the Great Plains, like *My Antonia* and *O Pioneers!*

88)

A Having set questions will help students read with the purpose of answering these questions.

89)

D Writing that has unity contains only information directly related to the thesis and topic sentences.

90)

D While checking on students' understanding and progress is important, this strategy does not help students grasp content material; it only helps the teacher evaluate where her students are in the learning process.

91)

A Universal screening is *part* of a response to intervention (RtI) or multi-tiered system of supports (MTSS) framework (which also includes other elements). Universal screening is the process by which all students are proactively screened for possible difficulties.

92)

D Susan B. Anthony says that she wants to prove she has the right to vote, which is an attempt to convince others.

93)

A, D Susan B. Anthony rhetorically asks, "The only question left to be settled now is: Are women persons?"

Amplification is the repetition of a word or expression for emphasis. The words *persons* and *citizens* are repeated throughout the speech to encourage audience members to consider the meanings of these important terms.

94)

C A slippery slope argument occurs when one assumes that a series of occurrences will happen as a result of a particular action or event.

95)

C The Iowa Test of Basic Skills is a single assessment tool used in multiple schools throughout the nation.

96)

B Giving students strategies, such as the SQ3R method, to help them comprehend a difficult text can be helpful across the content areas.

97)

B Speakers use inflection, by changing tone or pitch, to show changes in meaning or attitude.

98)

C The transition word *finally* indicates the end of a sequence.

99)

C Preteaching new vocabulary is a best practice in this situation since it will give students more confidence and self-efficacy as they tackle this difficult text.

100)

C "Medical practitioners must learn to be sensitive with people who are in crisis" is an adequate summary of the passage overall. The other options only provide specific details from the passage.

Follow the link below to take your second ILTS English Language Arts (207) practice test and to access other online study resources:

www.cirrustestprep.com/ilts-ela-online-resources